Praise for "No

"Now the Dance has
Lotten Säfström's de
to Dance".

In "Now the Dance has Begun" the author recounts what
has happened in her life since she stopped using alcohol.
She describes the challenges she faces in everyday life.

Liberally and without lecturing, she tells us about her
new way of life, sharing samples and personal reflections on what it is like to have a permanent place to live,
and to be a "reborn" parent. She also talks of how she is
beginning to learn how to manage rudimentary daily
chores at the age of 39.

The book is highly recommend to all categories of read-
ers, whether they have a link with people experiencing
addiction or not.

This is a useful, heartfelt and humorous book about how
it is to be human.

Maria Bielke von Sydow,
    Author and Publisher

————

At the age of 39, the Swedish writer, Lotten Säfström, stepped out into reality after a life scarred by her dependency to alcohol and other drugs.

She has documented the hardships caused by addiction and her journey back to life in two exceptionally well-written books, which have already become minor classics in her home-country.

"I Only Wanted to Dance" is as exciting as "On the road" by Kerouac. This first, mad leg of her life's journey is authentic and, incredibly, she survives it all.

The sequel, "Now the Dance has Begun" is full of insight and experience, not only to those who are affected in the aftermath of drug-abuse or those recovering from the disease of addiction, but to anybody who has encountered difficulties in life.

Two exciting novels on a universal subject!

Elisabeth Brännström,
    Author, Columnist and Literary Critic

Praise for "I Only Wanted to Dance":

This is a strong narrative that should be of interest to most people. A book that even youngsters ought to read, so that they never become seduced by romanticized descriptions of narcotics or alcohol.

(Citation from booklet #12121088)
Pia Holmström, Reader, BTJ, the Swedish Library Service

This book is, first and foremost, very important as it deals with many aspects of addiction. It tells an engaging true story of a tough fight battling this disease, its many faces and its deceitful progression.

But, it is also a book about awakening, surrendering and finding a way out.

Filled with empathy and educational importance.

Wonderfully written and beautifully executed.

Peter Nilsson
BSc Medical Biology and Chemistry

Lotten's book "I Only Wanted to Dance" is an honest and well-written book about the progression of addiction and, most of all, about the painful path into a balanced recovery. Lotten gives life to the addicted parent's role and also portrays her love for her child. The narrative ought to be of solace to other parents and of benefit to social workers in search of solutions to help the children of addicts.

The book moved me deeply, I cried about some and was gladdened by the others of the phases in Lotten's life.

Everyone who comes into contact with addiction, whether within the family or in a professional capacity, has something to learn from Lotten's story. The book is all the more readable thanks to its strong narrative style and vivid language.

Thank you, Lotten, for having the courage to share your and your child's life with us. Best regards to you both!

Eva Edstedt,
Former Manager at Malin's Minne

About the Author

Lotten Säfström, born May 16th 1966 in Borlänge, Sweden, is an author, lecturer and publisher.

She is based at her own company, Salto De Vita.

Her life's work is to be part of the widespread movement of people around the world who are trying to learn what causes addiction and, most importantly, how to create a life-style that makes staying free of mind-altering substances more attractive than relapsing.

In her own words: "It is very important for professionals to research the physical and psychological hows and whys of this deadly affliction. For the victims in the wake of substance-abuse, though, a crucial thing is learning how people who have this disorder can begin to live a life where relapse does not become an option. Victims of addiction are also the children, relatives, friends and those devastated by crimes committed by abusers of alcohol and other drugs. We already know how to diagnose this deadly, and in so many ways, harmful disorder in the very early stages of its progression. Now, an even stronger focus needs to be put on continuing to implement this knowledge, in order to develop further the strategies that will decimate the awfully high numbers of those who suffer because of addiction."

Lotten is also an advocate for bringing education about healthy emotional development into school in order to give future generations a ground-breaking head start in personal health and adult responsibility.

The authors' books "I Only Wanted to Dance" and "Now the Dance has Begun" are written with the intention of relaying support, solace and hopefully inspiration to those living, caring for or working in the proximity of people with an addictive disorder.

Her literary works may also be of interest to people who have found the desire to give up that lifestyle and will, possibly interest those who are still suffering from active addictive patterns.

These books are written for adults but, with adult supervision, teenagers can benefit from reading them too.

Now the Dance has Begun

by

Lotten Säfström

Salto de Vita

Published by Salto De Vita, 2016

info@saltodevita.com

© Lotten Säfström 2016

Proofreading: Suzannah Young and Katja Hjelm

Cover Illustration: Limpo Rocha

Typesetting: Nanna Salemark

Print: Booksfactory, Poland, 2016

ISBN: 978-91-983173-1-2

To my beloved family and fellow travellers!

With wishes of
keeping our desires on a fruitful evolution for humanity and
our world -
to always encourage the upcoming generations to surpass
us.

All the love and courage to us all on our path.

Preface

My main intentions with the books, "I Only Wanted to Dance" and "Now the Dance has Begun", have been to contribute to the discussion on the possibilities for recovery, both from co-dependency and from addiction to alcohol, which was my drug of choice, and also to other mind-altering chemicals. Recovery from the harm caused by substance abuse.

Since "I Only Wanted to Dance" was published, the things I have learned and shared with others have brought me beyond that initial intention. The esteem I have gained for our humanity and our world is limitless.

Also, the understanding that humanity is taking its first, tentative baby-steps on the path of behavioural science has been heartening. With this understanding, I need to be very open-minded about what works in healing the mind and spirit of a person. In my experience, much comes gradually and from within.

But, in the beginning, I had to be helped by others. I needed to become aware that accepting help is a good thing. To ask for help is to be strong.

To take part in what has worked for other humans has proven itself to be an intelligent and loving action to safeguard my very life. This has, in turn, benefitted the wellbeing of my child and other people around me.

Thanks to my taking responsible action for my ongoing recovery, I can finally be a resource to others.

I am so grateful to the person who called the police when I was drunk with my daughter Emma, who was two years old at the time, and in my care. Without that person sounding the alarm on how ill I was, I would not be alive today. The social services took this seriously and stood by our side until I became well enough to take care of my child. Otherwise, Emma would probably have developed and passed on this social dysfunction to the next generation in our family tree as well.

Another intention with these books is to tell a tale of gratitude, trust and hope.

I look back at the years that have passed and the words are so many. They shout out to be written. To fill page after page, volumes full of all we have done, everything that has happened and all the work we've put in.

I have listened and now they will be told. At least the ones that stand out, pleading to be written.

This book is also published to tell a narrative. Despite the fact that this is a tale of the mind and spirit, it is also a most practical journey. It is only through doing that I am able to heal and evolve.

This is an account of recovery, a process which doesn't miraculously fall into my lap.

I have been free from using any intoxicating substances since 11th March 2006 but this freedom is something I can't take for granted. I still have, and will have for life, an addictive personality. My ambition is always to make my sober life more attractive than the drunken one was.

I need to take care of myself in order to be able to take care of others. Being a parent brings that fact to the peak of its truth. To the peak of responsibility for living and being present.

I need to understand who I am in order to understand another person. After all, we aren't that different at the core.

The only crux is that if I were to tell it all in a chronological manner, this would be the longest autobiography in the history of the genre. Loads and loads get done when Emma and I are absorbed in living. It's all in, all at once. Everything that can be felt, processed and created.

So I have decided to write this book in topic-related chapters. A tale of a family life that began for a five-year-old and a 40-year-old at a swirling pace in January 2007.

I begin this book by inviting You, Dear Reader, to join

me on the adventurous expedition that I first set foot on ten years ago. This path of planting my roots in the established order of things.

Prologue

Oh, wondrous reality! The little Krill had come home! Lately, the longing for her had become beyond painful to bear since I had found my way into sobriety ten months earlier. This state of constantly missing her had been my emotional companion since Emma had moved from our home to the orphanage in November 2005. And then my parental instinct had begun to take on a healthy form when I stopped using alcohol. Healthy and so much stronger.

Much of my understanding about the nature of my disease came from seeing how I had let a drug come between me and my child. I had never understood how ill I was before, while I was still getting drunk.

On the 2nd of January 2007, the doors of the elevator whirred open on our floor and out ran the little bubble of life. She made a sprinting start straight for me and I spread out my arms, catching her mid-air. Radiating at me, with her huge smile and eyes twinkling, she kissed me, over and over, the peals of her adorable laughter echoing in the stairwell.

"Yes!!! Finally, little Krill! Finally!", I cried while smiling at least as broadly back at her.

Loaded with bags and suitcases, Mona and Ulf stood happily beaming while watching us and when Emma and I managed to let go of each other, it was their turn for big hugs.

"Aren't you joining us inside for a bit? There are cookies and drinks for everybody..."

They shook their smiling heads in unison.

"Cookies!? And drinks!? Well, come on then, Mummy. We'll be going then. See you. Bye!"

The whirlwind waved at Mona and Ulf but her eyes were locked on the hallway, as if she had laser eyes, straight through walls into the kitchen.

"Oh, no you don't! Now we say our proper goodbyes. Mona and Ulf will be leaving in a minute. Come back here."

"This is your moment", Mona said, with tears of joy in her eyes. "To think that you actually made it, Lotten!"

She hugged me as if she never wanted to let go and I mumbled:

"Thanks for everything. What you have given us..." We both drew in deep, rasping breaths.

"Yeah, yeah," Ulf pulled me free, "We haven't even started giving yet! Come here and give us a hug so we can leave you two to more important things. The child craves the sugar!"

"Yeah-Absolutely!" Came the reply in a micro-second from the little wad in Mona's arms.

Everybody embraced everybody and after confirming that we would be seeing each other soon, the elevator doors whirred shut and my child and I stood in the stairwell looking at each other. That moment felt like an eternity to me, but was probably only a few hundredths of a second. The magic bubble was popped by the metre or so of child who restlessly blurted:

"Where's the party, Mummy?" After me doing the Charlie Chaplin eyebrows, we burst into giggles and I swooped her up, twirling us around and around, whooping.

"Right here, darling! Right here!"

We carried all her stuff inside, closed our front door and there our family life began. In our first real home. Together.

Part One

The Habitat

Two bedrooms, a living room, a kitchen and a super-cute minimal conservatory, all on the ninth floor. Two shared laundry rooms and an enormous yard that was one floor above street-level and so was safe for children. It felt so unreal.

After 22 years of homelessness, where I'd lived alternately inside and outside, all the while beyond the reaches of a healthy social context, suddenly having a home was an existential shock.

Of course, everything in life was new to me because I was experiencing the world without mind-altering substances for the first time in 25 years, but living, being responsible, making this commitment to a fixed habitat, really felt almost surreally new.

During the years of addiction, when my drug of choice had been foremost alcohol, deranged theories concerning my homelessness had translated into me being a "free spirit". Boasting about not being caught up in the co-hell-ision, a pun I made up to ridicule the 'coalition' of mankind. All my theories had been vague utopian defences against living as I did. In reality, I had never been "free to roam the Earth" since my addiction had taken precedence over every healthy habit and chained me to the availability of and my search for drugs. The only free spirits were the ones stolen from liquor stores.

Through the years, there had been a few occasions when I'd painted myself into a corner and had had to seek aid from people in the "ruled" world, but this had only been to get me through whatever ongoing crisis I'd wound up in. My goal had always been to manipulate people so I got what I needed very effectively and then be able to move on, away from the risk of being touched by normalcy, as soon as possible. I had been unable to accept half-way compromises. To live with one foot in and the other outside the established "world of disorder" was not for me.

I had followed only the impulse to use alcohol which demanded that I live an uncommitted lifestyle. I was blind to the realisation that, as the years went by, this impulse cried louder and louder, tethering me down harder and harsher than any other path could. And it expected my very life in return. Freedom and choice had never, ever been factors in this equation.

With regards to our new home, my logical thought-patterns told me that it was now, bound to a lease, that I was getting to have actual freedom of choice over my whole life. But my old emotional pattern of being a cornered animal still gnawed at me with the feeling of being trapped.

As soon as I became sober, I asked to be allowed back on the after-care programme of Malin's Minne, the treatment centre my daughter Emma and I had been to. They were very happy to have me back and now Emma could finally come with me, joining in the children's group where she was looked after by staff from the children's care team at the Malin's Minne centre. This became the trip we both looked forward to most each week. For Emma, it was seeing old and new friends and grown-ups from her daily routines back when we lived there. For me, it was the 'getting-outta-Dodge', always the travel-ler, getting an emotional breather from home as soon as we left for the train station, but it was also an extremely important part of my recovery process.

Sitting in this group therapy session with women just like me, I had the opportunity to talk about everything that had been happening since Emma and I had moved into our home. The other mothers laughed about the things I talked about, but they weren't laughing at me, they laughed with me. They knew. Living without ever being intoxicated was like living in another world.

Even though I had gotten an incredibly nice apartment, I still had a gnawing, uneasy feeling inside and the oth-ers' empathetic laughter and baffled comments about my disproportionate sensation of discomfort helped me get some perspective. The group's therapist of the group mentioned that I had actually never had a home before, in my entire life. I stared at her, emotionally numbed, silently letting her words sink in. I had moved for the first time when I was four months old and, up until now, I had moved 65 times. The sixteen homes I'd had as a child, the fleeting subletting of apartments and houses, the using or "taking care" of other people's places and the eight times I moved the caravan – and that wasn't counting all the bushes and stairwells.

Seen in this light, the mystery of my feeling uncomfortable in this new situation suddenly didn't appear strange at all and after that particular session I had yet another thing to use as a reminder and booster when I felt awkward.

From time to time, in unexpected bursts, an overwhelming gratitude for my home would surface and drown all the uncomfortable emotions, and so it kept on coming in waves of strong, impulsive emotions.

At home, I would look at Emma being all comfy, padding around in her home, having all sorts of projects going on or seeing her simply just sitting around doing nothing, and then I would try to muster this homely feeling within myself. More often than not, I would realise that I was walking around, restlessly, carrying the weight of guilt about not being worthy of such a beautiful habitat. Then I would try to tell myself that I did too have the right to live like this, but often that didn't work. Then I could always fall back on turning the dread into gratefulness for my child having and loving her home. That method would always let me enjoy myself for a bit.

Those were very odd times, indeed.

I went to many meetings in my self-help organisation. There were lunch meetings I could attend when Emma was at the day-care centre. When I shared about what was happening in my life, the subject of habitation was something that came up again and again.

Intellectually, I could see that the discomfort was a result of my being born into rootlessness but emotionally, that theory never seemed to hit the nail on the head. A slithering restlessness relentlessly squirmed under the surface. I had to trust that I would one day be able to find peace and rest in our home and focus on my pure gratitude for my sobriety instead.

The idea that the wheres and whys of my discomfort had many roots was evidently too multifaceted to grasp fully.

March came upon us and our lives had begun to run to a sort of routine. My restlessness shone through with us having to have activities every day after I picked Emma up. One day she had dance-class, the next day we went to the public baths, one day there was a parental guidance course where Emma partook in another children's group and then there were the after-care sessions where we had to take the train to a place 50 minutes out of Malmö - and for the remaining three days I always had some kind of excursion planned.

One late afternoon, after three months of this constant "doing something", Emma stood, fully dressed in the hallway as we were on our way out, as usual. Suddenly, she looked up at me with a pleading look and, in a tone drained of all strength, the bubble burst:

"Mommy, please! Can't we just stay home today? Pleeease!!!" She almost started to cry.

My whole world crashed down. In an instant, I saw what these last winter months had looked like to her, with the never-ending outings. My voice scarcely carried my reply:

"Well, eh, well, of course, my dearest darling... But, eh, what, uh, what shall we do then...?"

Her whole being shone up and, tilting her head, with a huge smile, she almost laughed the words that just spear-pointed my soul:

"Why, nothing at all, Mommy! We'll just sit, do nothing and watch the telly."

Then she almost tore her jacket off, as if to outrun me, if I was about to change my mind.

Emotionally, I gaped quietly at her, maybe I actually let my chin drop. I felt like one would feel seeing an alien being. "What does she mean, "do nothing, just sit?!"

Hesitantly, brow furrowed, I began hanging up our

coats in a surging, panicky state. I had no idea whatsoever what to "do at home". I brought a book from my bedside table, which I tried to get sucked into, but even reading, which had always been my refuge earlier in life, escaped me. My concentration abandoned me. I looked at Emma being cosy, fiddling with little fiddlings wherever she went, or at her just sitting somewhere in the flat and I tried to assimilate that atmosphere of presence into myself but my progress was not noticeable. I actually found the state of "just being" quite agonising and it was all but impossible for me.

Sure, we stayed home a bit more often after this, but I still kept up this dragging us out for some kind of excursion almost daily.

When we stopped doing as many activities as before, I found another way to escape from being in the here and now. I fell "in love". Now I could go about homely things, all the while absorbed in turbulent dream scenarios of this guy and "doing nothing" suddenly became much more manageable. But I wasn't truly present, neither for Emma nor myself.

There was never any actual development between me and the chosen one, but during the ten days this obsession lasted, I at least managed to ask him if he had any plans on having more children. His shocked expression, the fact that he instantly raised one hand in a stop-sign, took two physical steps backwards while shaking his head firmly, stating,

"No, no! No, no, no!", definitely helped me wake up from that escape from reality.

It was actually very lucky for me that this person wasn't interested in a relationship. What I labelled as being love was no more than an addictive reaction – a strong symptom of my desperate impulse to flee.

When spring arrived and it was legitimate to be outside all the time, my relief was immeasurable! I bought a small barbecue that fit into my bicycle basket and we "ate out" a lot during the next six months of warmth. To tell the truth, I also put it to good use in the winter...

At the meetings, I kept on coming back to the topic of my inability to settle down. I repeated over and over that this was because of my never having had a long-lasting home. The yearning for movement and action hurt inside.

I became more and more aware that I was abnormally drawn to having something radical and turbulent happening in my daily life. An idea would sneak up on me and I was suddenly caught up in thoughts, feelings and actions that absorbed all my energy. The extent to which my energy got involved surprised me. Even to be able to perform normal activities without having them take over my entire existence did not come naturally to me.

I seldom did anything moderately.

Fervently I practiced spiritual and physical tools to attain much needed serenity. I had to sit down, breath and inwardly "talking and listening" in my spiritual way of practice, to let my thoughts and feelings come and go – what I simply called prayer and meditation. If I noticed that I needed more than that to disperse my self-centredness I would call someone to get a perspective. I would also get a wonderful inner peace by exercising, especially when riding my bicycle.

When I looked back at the first ten months of my sobriety, I could clearly see how much energy I had put into the longing and struggling, and finally the organising of everything, so that Emma could move back in with me. Now that the deep hole of missing my child had been filled and the worry over finding a good home for us had been eliminated, I realised that I had believed that I would be completely content with life as soon as those two goals had been achieved. Now it became evident that living to daily routine, something I had dreamed of, turned up new and previously unforeseen needs which needed tending to, all the time.

Thankfully, in the midst of my constant and undefined, gnawing restlessness, I found comfort in this revelation – life would never get boring!

Unpacking our stuff took time. Strangely, I felt like I didn't dare empty the boxes. In my earlier life, I had always had to move when a place had begun to feel homely and cosy. That chain of events had never altered. With my family, I'd had no influence over our moving from home to home. But, from the age of thirteen, when I had decided to go live at boarding school and thus moving away from my family in Saudi Arabia where we had lived at the time, pulling up my roots became a pattern in my life.

Mostly, the sensation of being cornered was what usually sent me packing. I could have created a terrible drunken chaos that got me evicted or that simply made me leave of my own accord. A few times, there had been other outer factors that had forced my hand and kept me on the move – a tent that had gotten stolen, the time when my and my boyfriend's caravan had caught fire, another time the owner of the apartment I was living in had returned suddenly and needed to move back in early, or simply a short-term lease that had expired.

Now it was a very different situation for me. I wasn't going to follow the insane impulses which my addiction had led me to and my lease was a secure one, but the fear of impending doom and chaos still echoed its well-known, oft-repeated refrain in my subconscious. If I got unpacked and everything got too snuggly, out I would be.

I went past the tiny conservatory and cast long side-glances through the glassed door. There, I had piled up

boxes and bags. In September 2004, before I was off to the
first period of rehab in early December, I had been given
an eviction notice for the 1st January 2005. By that time,
I had received three warnings over the two years we had
lived there. All of them about unacceptable disturbance
in the flat which my mother had rented for Emma and
me. I went to the treatment centre and I was in such a
terrible physical and mental state that I hadn't been able
to empty the apartment, not even to stow any of our stuff.

My addiction to alcohol was so grave that I hadn't been
able to keep the day-to-day things afloat towards the end.
My family was incredibly loving and, despite the fact
that they weren't able to talk to me or have me around
because of my always being intoxicated, they helped me
with this move even though I wasn't even there to help
in person. They had packed, thrown out lots of junk and
worn-out things and stored some of what I owned in my
sister's barn. They even cleaned the flat so that I wouldn't
get a fine from the landlord.

Now all I had to show for my 40 years of life on this Earth
was packed in a few boxes and some bags. The thought of
having to look into them was not appealing. The memories of how those last few months had been - or actually
it was those last few years after Emma's birth - haunted
me, and they did so with terrifying force and depth.

I glanced in and touched on the thought of clearing

up the stacks of things, but a wall of reluctance arose inside me and just the thought of it caused a stab which wrenched my gut. I kept putting off this chore, again and again.

When autumn began poking its nose into summer's business, I had to make a decision. I couldn't stand the idea of the winter months coming and me not having cleared out these triggers of agonising memories. My guilty conscience and the lurking memories would suffocate me during the long dark months of winter. I made a decision to empty one box a week.

I rolled up my sleeves and set my focus on the gratitude I felt. I remember targeting my thankfulness toward the person who had notified the police about me being drunk in public when Emma was with me, which had led to our little family going to the treatment centre, which led to Emma and me having gotten our lives on the right track. In the loving spirit of contemplating this miraculous chance at living a waking dream, I then had only to dig in.

Teletubbies movies that had gone on and on throughout many of Emma's waking hours. The sight of them brought her voice back to me. The many times when she had called out from her loneliness, needing help to put in a new video cassette when I had been lying down, ridden with the terrible lows of being in awful mental or physical states. Memories of my alcohol dosages which didn't do me any good anymore.

A children's book from the library that had never gotten read. Even though I'd had it a whole year before we were dropped off at the treatment centre. Here it was, not even returned, reminding me of all the fantasies I'd had of raising my daughter. All the plans in my head that were never made real.

Kitchen appliances filled three whole boxes. Actually, I had used one pan for Emma's pasta and, one frying pan for fish sticks, meatballs and sausages. All the other things had just been décor. The memories of how I hardly ever ate rushed into me.

A favourite sweater that told tales of the trails between the different liquor stores. At the bottom of one box lay a camouflage-bottle – a sports water bottle I used to fill with alcohol in the various public toilets all over town. The times at the playgrounds when Emma had begged me to play with her and I had replied, "Just a minute. Just let me smoke this cigarette. I can't right now. Wait. Soon..."

To call this "a difficult task" would be just the tip of the ice-berg of these overwhelming emotions.

When the first box was empty, I did not keep to the plan but drove myself to empty several more. I shouldn't have done. The psychological fatigue that hit me floored me and afterwards I couldn't resume this task for weeks.

My guilty conscience ate at me all my waking hours, but instinctively I pushed back doing it again as hard as I could. To confront the raw pain of what our lives had truly been like was just too brutal. This would have to happen in its own time.

I was on a mentally- and emotionally crazed roller-coaster between heaven and Earth with all the difficult memories bringing feelings of anguish mixed in with the day-to-day worries about doing the right thing for us both. But even in the midst of this sense of being a lost cause, feeling such difficult sorrow and frustration, life was still better than it had ever been. Gratitude was something I was very good at mustering. Also, the trust at wondrously having found my rightful place in life brought a soaring sense of joy. Emma and I had lots of fun every day, and at the twelve-step recovery meetings there was always something I heard which lifted my spirit. The difficulties were rendered quite harmless, and even turned into useful tools, because I was able to summon them to help me think about the overall wonder of my new way of life.

It was an extremely important and incredibly brave thing for me to accept the help of others. Everything to be able to act differently than just blindly following the deep and habitual impulse to flee. And not just to flee geographically – not being part of a social setting had been a full-time job for me before, even in the company of others. Even living together with someone had not meant that I experienced togetherness.

I realised that I was often caught up in making detailed plans to get away from the here and now. It was like an instinct. I had to begin the practice of putting my mental feet down in the moment. The best result was achieved through gratitude and trusting that there was enough adventure for now. I reminded myself that I had many and unforeseeable inner and outer journeys in my future. Life right now was an anthill of miracles, happenings that I never could have predicted, so I leaned against that fact as a crutch to aid me while I breathed deeply, physically and mentally, gradually simmering down.

Creating a stable and positive sense of hearth and home was literally a cornerstone of my survival. Thankfully I had other sober people to turn to. It wasn't really "just stopping" using mind-altering substances. I had to change everything and at the same time create a fulfilling daily life. Stable, loving and rich days to fortify my zero tolerance toward the alcohol and other drugs.

I had begun going to therapy sessions on the addiction ward at the hospital. There, I got a lot of perspective about what could be "normal" worries about maintaining a home and what troubles could be symptoms of my addictive disorder.

"I haven't cleaned the floors since last week and I don't think I polished the windows at all last month. It feels like it's piling up. Well, it's not sickeningly dirty or anything, but aren't you supposed to clean at least once a week and do the windows minimum once every month? Or are you?"

Pleading, my soul sweating, I searched my therapist's face for clues. Throughout my life, I hadn't had friends with homes that they valued and whom I could have gathered hints from. I didn't have a clue as to how most people went about these kinds of things.

She actually guffawed.

"How do you think my husband and I would manage to keep such a routine with two small kids, long working hours and all our hobbies and activities? Sure, there are pedantic people out there but I don't know any and I'd rather have some dust bunnies in the corners than having to argue and stress out about keeping on like that.

You, who has so many pieces to puzzle together to create a homely atmosphere for Emma and yourself, with all your activities and the importance of fitting in the basic daily routines. You really need to move down a gear, my dear!

A huge and dangerous hurdle for addicts that become sober is wanting too much, too quickly. Minimize the must-dos to sheer essentials as best you can, that's my advice. Remind yourself often of the wonderful change you've made already and of what incredibly good work you put into your hours every day!"

Being given such reminders and praise were existential lifelines for me. For the first time since I was thirteen I had a home and I desperately wanted to keep it. I noticed that I had buried myself in catastrophic worries and carried them as far as nearly convincing myself that I would never be able to manage taking care of our flat. Thoughts haunted me of keeping the floor shiny under and behind the stove or else I would be evicted. Another was that if Emma didn't have a tidy play room everyone would think I was a terrible parent.

I told a friend about these mind-ghosts and she raised an eyebrow, asking:

"Who in Heaven's name has a tidy play room? Is that even healthy?" When she finished that sentence off with hearty laughter, I saw the light at the end of the tunnel. I began using these two people's responses to my fears as mantras.

My spontaneous thought-patterns of putting myself down kept popping up though. Some things I'd heard about the addictive disorder began echoing in my mind. The process of recovery seemed to be mostly a matter of learning to think and act in new ways. I now started to suspect that this meant getting into the habit of spotting when my disorder "took over my brain" with destructive impulses, rather than growing a saint-like personality. Any method was better than starting to use alcohol again. I would do anything to keep this freedom of choice! The voice telling me that I was unworthy would be smothered with love and inner reflection - not with drugs!

And then, as if the inner journey of coming to terms with being worthy of having living quarters wasn't enough, I met a new challenge. During the winter months that bordered on the one-year jubilee of us having our home, I was accused of being unworthy by outside forces.

We'd had an exhausting day, with a long walk on the beach and Emma already asked to be allowed to go to bed at 7 p.m.. After our evening routines with me reading to her, then some talking and snuggling, I went to lay down on the couch. Practising relaxing, I opened my book and, within an hour I was actually into the story. Thankfully, reading had started being enjoyable again more often. The clock had turned 9 when I heard something being dropped into the letter-box. I guessed it was some advertising leaflet or other and kept on reading until my eyelids signalled that it was time for bed.

When I was on my way to the bedroom, I passed the front-door and saw an envelope on the floor.

"Strange," I thought and opened it. Inside there was a

scribbled note:

"You must stop making noise. I beg. If you not stop I get you all throw out. You stampede like the elephant up there!"

I turned ice-cold. There was no sender. A feeling of "I've done it again!" poured over me. I was going to be evicted and this time despite not having done anything! In the back of my mind, a voice told me that it wasn't wrong, since I actually had stampeded quite a lot in my life, ruining the peace for many neighbours and land-lords in the past. Now it had all caught up with me in a karmic purgatory of righteous punishment. I felt a pounding cramp in my throat.

Then thoughts of Emma and her love of our home surfaced and my fears turned into rage in an instant. Of course, this emotional turmoil was not good for me either. It was my old way of reacting. I cursed the fools and their cousins with an intensity that made me physi-cally nauseous. All in the space of a few seconds.

I couldn't make sense of it. Hot bubbles of sorrow and anger fought for space with the fear within. The feelings I harboured were too strong for me and their fierceness scared me. The storm that erupted from those bubbles reminded me of how I had used to just pack up and flee. It hit me that good advice was hard to find and acutely necessary right now and it was too late to call anyone. I sat down to create a calm space inside of me and prayed for a solution to act on. I needed to resolve this situation and tone down this inner storm.

Eventually, some kind of sanity was restored. It had taken almost an hour and the balance was not entirely stable. I got hold of a pen and frantically noted some points down.

We had not been noisy.

We hadn't been at home all day.

When we had gotten home we had had dinner and put Emma, the walking sleepy-head, to bed. Early!

I had been on the couch all evening (thank God!)

This helped a bit. But what to do now?

The answer hit me at once: Attack is the best defence!

Firstly, I decided on calling the landlord first thing next morning. Then I wrote a note that I taped to the wall in the elevator.

I had to rewrite it several times. The words became more readable and less aggressive with every draft and, finally, I was satisfied. I pointed out that we hadn't been loud, that we hadn't been at home all day and that I would contact the landlord the next day. I also asked them to call in a disturbance complaint instead of accusing us in this manner. "Then the professionals can come over and you will find out which tenant is really the one who is disturbing you!"

I still had a hard time falling asleep that night and in the morning I called the landlord as soon as their offices opened. I was given reassurance that no one had called or reported anything to them and they asked me to contact them at once if this happened again or if I found out who was behind the note I had received. I told them that as a family with a small child of course there was playing and mischief-making about the house, but never for a long time or unusually often. They told me to call again if these people accused us of anything again, and I did.

Within two weeks, they came to my door for the first time. I called the landlord's office and was told that they knew of this family and that this wasn't the first time they had bothered their neighbours.

Six months of unpleasantness followed – angry comments when we met in the elevator, more angry notes, coming to our door - and when one of the family members shouted at Emma when she was alone and six years old at the time, the last drop was spilled. The landlord finally intervened and gave them an official reprimand, not me...

A very strange thing was that these neighbours managed to time their accusations exactly at times when we really hadn't been at home or had had unusually quiet evenings. This was very fortunate because it helped the processing of my catastrophic fears of being evicted. I still felt very bad though - the oozing worry wouldn't subside completely. Despite seeing the logical facts in these situations and having the landlord completely on our side.

At first, I didn't share about this at the therapy or meetings. Not even with my twelve-step sponsor. I carried it within me and thought I ought to overcome this intellectually. The circumstances of our innocence were logical and apparent and also, we had had reassurances from the landlord that we had nothing to fear. But rationalising didn't work. Finally, I couldn't stand the brooding and gave in. I brought it up with my sponsor, even though it made me feel like a fool.

She told me of a similar situation that had befallen her when she had gotten a dog. Her landlord had reassured her by saying that those who wanted to live in a silent house should buy one in the countryside. After this conversation, it took a day or two and then the obsessive mind games vanished completely.

After having had these fears for such a long time, I don't really know how or why they eased off so quickly after our talk, but I did get a deeper understanding of the importance of speaking up and airing whatever was harassing my brain. No matter how worldly or silly something might seem to me, my disorder uses eroding and harmful thoughts and gets in the way of my well-being in recovery. I talked about such recurring, irritating thoughts more often in the future, regardless of how I imagined I would look in other people's eyes. I couldn't afford to harbour such resentments.

Between the ages of one-and-a-half and four years of age, I lived in the same house in Gävle. That was the longest I'd lived anywhere in my entire life. Now this has been my home for many times longer than that. The drama surrounding our home ended with that one feud and now we are one of the families that have lived here the longest.

They came knocking one last time and then I dared to show them how angry I was:

"Now, here and now, this ends! Either you come in here and we'll all go watch my daughter sleeping quietly or else you will just leave. Right now! In the future, you will make the disturbance call – I will not have you slipping notes in our letterbox or ringing the doorbell anymore! And if you dare speak to my little girl again I will report you to the authorities!"

This was wonderfully refreshing and since then we have been left alone.

When I had defended my habitats in my homeless years I'd rarely had any right to them and the complaints had almost always been more than justified. Now my unwanted but enforced feud with the neighbours had given well-needed nourishment to my inexperienced and tentative roots. I got a better foothold in my newfound role as a settler in the world. This fight to defend our home led to unexpected positive personal growth. The homely sense of "my habitat" had gotten manyfold stronger. The fact that I had stood up for my integrity made me grow both as a human being and, above all, as a worthy citizen.

The years in our home linger on. Sorting the boxes took a long, long time. I decided to put some of them in the storage space we have in the basement – some were actually not sorted until 2015 – eight years after we moved in...

That the unpacking would play such a big part in the therapeutic processing of my old way of life was something I hadn't counted on. The tears and remorse that always come when I look through things from our insane past have helped me to heal and explain some of the inexplicable things I did back then. I walked on through, carrying out these chores of anguish, and became a more whole person from it.

Every now and then, I become obsessed with the thought of moving abroad or moving somewhere else within my city. My empty, craving space inside shouts that moving is what I need to do to give Emma and me a richer life. My longing for something else and something extraordinary will always look for new channels within me but the impulse to flee, a symptom of the disease of addiction, will not be what chases me from one place to another again.

I have learned to look out for this lie and see it, eventually, if not at once. As long as I take care of myself and my recovery, I will come out on the other side of this loud yearning and keep on inhabiting our beautiful home. When the attacks pass, I realise that this home is the most fantastic alternative I have. Then I feel true, clear joy at being rooted in this world.

At least I get to change the insides of our location. We have redecorated lots of times.

In the beginning, everything we owned were either gifts or bought at second-hand stores. Recently, I bought new curtains for the first time but I still buy at second-hand, both for economic and environmental reasons.

The style of our home has gone from cluttered "having-no-idea-what-so-ever" to simple but rather modern. I must admit that this is largely thanks to my fiancé who has a very good eye for these things.

The process of feeling like I am home is still ongoing for me and differs from day to day and moment to moment. Seconds have become minutes, minutes half-hours and, nowadays, there can be longer periods of undisrupted cosiness.

It is a marvellous feeling, this wonder of "being at home".

It is a miracle that I have a fixed coordinate on the face of the Earth! And the inner perpetuum mobile is a constant in our family so life never gets boring.

My desire is to go on valuing my habitat, to root myself deeper and keep on enjoying having my own home. Even if I do move some day.

Body

Incredibly, I have survived!

Only a few weeks before I stopped using alcohol, my doctor told me that my liver was comparable to that of an 80-year-old active alcoholic. In other words, I did not have much time left on this Earth.

What got to me the most, even though I tried to ignore it with all my might, was my doctor's attitude when she told me the news. She sounded resigned for the first time since I had first met her four years previously. She was South American and actually had that stereotypical fiery, emotional way of communicating. She had vividly shown anger, desperation and been in-my-face before, but during this appointment she didn't even sound sad. A resigned spirit carried her words.

"You are killing yourself. In a few months, your body will no longer be able to break down the alcohol. Knowing this and continuing to use alcohol is the same thing as taking your own life."

I didn't stop using but this scare was one of the important pieces of the mosaic that brought me to a conclusion about my addiction.

I had minimized the fact that I had played with Death since I was fifteen and now someone had said that ugly truth out loud. Unbelievably, throughout my entire life, no one had explicitly expressed the suicidal aspect of the disease of addiction to me before. In my deranged state, this had always whispered in the depths of my subconscious, but my destructive disorder just pushed the truth away with an emotional, "fuck it".

My doctor's words, now finally spoken by someone, kept echoing in my head. The tone of her voice haunted me those last mad and eternal weeks of using.

As soon as I became sober I went to have new test samples taken to assess how badly my body had been damaged. The wait for the results was more than unbearable. The amazing and miraculous change of perception which freedom from intoxication brought, the reality I now experienced, brought with it a euphoric sense of a need to live. To co-exist and to share this love of life with Emma and others. It was as if I could breathe existence. My life had quickly begun to reverse from the confinement of both body and mind and the emotional stress I had known since my teens.

The yearning for living in "this world" was now so strong that even if it was death that awaited around the next corner, I would still stay on the path of this mental liberation. The gratitude to get to have lived like this at all, the most free I had ever been, was enormous.

I went to the addiction ward every day of the week, of my own volition, because I needed to have an anchor outside of my self-help program. I was amazed at staying clean and was very careful to keep an airtight bubble around me.

One day, as I sat in the patient area waiting to give one of the regular tests to confirm that I was still sober, my doctor approached me. I greeted her and she, back to her old fiery self again, blurted out with a very grave expression:

"Aaah, Lotten! You have to come with me now! Into my room at once. It is very important!"

She rushed on, beckoning to me to follow. I was ushered onto a stool in front of her desk, with her giving me a very serious look:

"You have to sit down. I have the results of your liver tests. You had better sit down!"

She clicked several times on the mouse and, stony-faced, she rotated the screen my way. I felt a sinking feeling in my gut that weighed as heavy as a boulder and a lump in my throat began throbbing painfully. She told me to look, pointing her pen at indecipherable curves and figures. I could hardly see at all for the tears in my eyes.

"Look here!" She repeated, tapping the screen, smiling eagerly, which collided with the terror I felt.

"Look at this! I have never seen anything like it! The condition of your liver is nearly perfect! I have never seen improvement this quick before! In one month, it has recovered to almost normal standards for a woman your age! How has this happened? How is it possible?!"

It took several endless seconds for this to sink in. I stared wordlessly at her from the sea of death-angst and at first I didn't understand a word she was saying. In my mind, I was thinking about Emma, wondering how she was going to cope. In the depths of sorrow over how my monstrous life had brought us to this, and then suddenly to the collision with the doctor's words. I literally had to shake my head to understand what she was going on about. It was as if I was watching a movie-frame where her lips moved and the sounds were distorted, all hollow and indiscernible.

I managed to calm down and then I became angry. Couldn't she have looked a bit happier when she waved me into her office? During the last couple of minutes I had been sure that my time had come.

I didn't say anything. I couldn't speak. I landed, got my bearings and then I cried. Silently, I thanked the universe and the tears just flowed. I don't remember what else she said but whenever we meet she expresses, dramatically, her happiness and positive shock over my continued sobriety.

That time serves as a reminder of how my life could have ended. Recovery is not something I can take for granted. Maybe addicts in a hundred years will have the benefit of a more enlightened world, a deeper insight to the ruthlessness of the disease of addiction and into how we are able to recover – I sincerely hope so!

Ever since I was fourteen, and moved away from my family, I had stuffed my body with harmful chemical substances, mostly alcohol. I was caught in the delusion that this would make my life more fabulous but in truth the buzz served to deafen, more or less well, an emotional strain due to my social deficiency. When one substance didn't do what I wanted it to anymore, I changed drugs for a while or used several at once. My existence was devoted to glorifying my world with drugs – socially, party-wise, in "romantic" relationships or sitting and savouring tall glasses all by myself. Finally, every waking hour turned into a constant journey between possible moments where I could get the "joyous" opportunity to get intoxicated. Preferably without being disturbed or annoyed by killjoys.

To be without, to be content with experiencing life's highlights, challenges and grey zones whilst being my own, unfiltered self wasn't a factor I could even consider in my "reality". Dealing with pure emotions was not an alternative.

At the beginning of my life with alcohol, the discomfort I felt when I was sober was purely emotional and mental. A kind of relentless dissatisfaction and a gnawing sense of something missing. The yearning for the weekend was ever-present. The effects of alcohol blissfully took the edge off.

When my body had gotten used to this drug, a physical

misery also began to set in. Already in my teens I had strong symptoms of hangovers, but they weren't the ones one usually hears about. I never had headaches or felt nauseous. Rather it was like a restlessness crawling through my nervous system and a clear-voiced want for more – like when you get thirsty after having had a long work-out or on a hot day during a warm outing.

Many addicts are periodical users with varying lengths of abstinence and some are only focused on the weekends, when it is "allowed" and all the other days are just periods of waiting for Friday or holidays. But this is my story and I was very young when I realized that my thing was to keep an ongoing buzz. My addiction was to live life in a steady, utopian, tipsy state. On this illusion of what paradise on Earth looked like I built my life.

How would I learn to start caring for myself? How could I begin to create a lifestyle of healthy habits when I'd always been focused on poison being my booster? Without having to think about it twice, I knew I had a lot of new routines to learn and to use, to fill the empty void inside.

In learning to live my new life, the greatest feat was to value other people's experiences. It was also true related to the body. I began by listening a bit more focused at the meetings as soon as someone shared about healthy routines. I also asked around and talked a lot to my sponsor on the twelve-step program. That safe environment helped me boost my courage in such an important new area – instead of feeling paralysed, I felt hope and trust in doing what I heard from those who benefitted from regular exercise.

I soon came to understand the importance of endorphins, serotonin and a lot of other substances released into the body through exercise. These substances would help me keep a completely natural and beneficial "medication" flowing in my body. All in moderation of course. I began by making much use of my bicycle during the first year.

I wrote a long list of all the other health issues I had, listing them in order of importance:

Taking care of my dental health.
    Learning how to eat properly.
    Being 30 kilos overweight.
    Sleep.
    And, last but not least, came - Quitting smoking.

These were many areas and all very important. The most difficult ingredient for me was my lack of patience. I wanted to have all these pieces taken care of yesterday, but with grave seriousness I understood that I needed to be calm and allow a manageable pace if I was ever to get even one of these habits taken care of for the better. Juggling too many balls at once would put them all in danger of being dropped.

It was immensely helpful to check out other people's ways of organising their daily and weekly routines. Then I would weigh up the pros and cons and fit them into something that would suit me.

I surfed on the hope of life getting better as long as I let myself stay sober and have a loving goal set in my mind.

Teeth. During the autumn of my first year in recovery, I got my teeth in order thanks to the Swedish welfare system. This issue is regarded as an important process in the rehabilitation process of becoming a member of society.

After Emma and I had moved back in together, I could smile at our neighbours and at the staff at the daycare centre without having to hold back.

From having had toothaches and suffering much shame since I was a child, having had my first fillings done in Jordan, where I had moved with my family at the age of five. The liberation that came with healthy gums made me positively light-headed. Through the years, I had been sitting in emergency dental practices all over Sweden and in Jordan, also in Australia and Japan when I worked as a sailor and suffered terrible pain on several different occasions while en route back and forth across the Pacific Ocean. I remember especially one situation in Japan when the staff of the clinic formed a line to be able to get a look at my teeth. The Westerner with horrible teeth-status and the shock they expressed over the obvious signs of dental issues related to drug-abuse.

The torturous agony and caricature balloon cheeks were a health issue that no sane person would endure. The gratitude over this fills me daily, to this day.

Ever since my late teens, I had begged dentists to please surgically remove all my teeth, but the answer I got was always:

"No! Teeth are living organs!"

My interpretation of their unified resolve was that all dentists were disrespectful bullies. In my deranged state, the answer to this equation was that I would show them all by mistreating my teeth even more. This would be my revenge on the whole lot of them, proving my point until they did what I had told them was right from the beginning. That revenge was a truly harsh and horrific one – for me.

When the tough treatments were completed, I noticed the difference in how I was greeted in stores and met in social encounters. Probably, this perception lay more in my sense of self-regard than in others peoples' poor manners but I felt it.

I smile rather than not smiling, widely and quite often. Firstly because I am so eternally grateful for this new life, and then a little wider just because I finally can! More than once, people have told me they have seldom seen such a dazzling smile.

To finally have had this suffering dealt with strengthened my self-worth and this wondrous feeling kept me all the more motivated to keep on the path I had started down, and to put continuous effort into the other health-related topics on my list.

My abnormal impulse to break myself would not be allowed to reign over my well-being anymore! I wanted to live a life where I treated my body with love, respect and consideration. Both on the mental and emotional planes but most certainly on the physical too. I was very nervous about how I would be able to create an inspiring routine that would stand up in the long run. To see to my food habits and exercise would crave more effort than the couple of minutes I needed for cleaning my teeth, and not taking care of all these things was just not an option.

Food. Endless, uncharted reaches into cluelessness. Trying to find a feasible path among the trillions of suggestions, different approaches and factions I had heard about in this area was something I quickly had to abandon. Here, my intuition became my truest instrument. I contemplated the dishes I heard and found out about through my searches, then my gut feeling was the guide I followed to decide if I was going to try to cook something or not. To be 40 years old and not have the slightest idea of what I liked to serve at home was to face an exciting and sometimes overwhelming challenge.

During my first ten months sober, I lost ten of the 25 kilos I had set as a final goal. This was a very different timescale concerning weight-loss compared to earlier in life. Then, I could gain or lose ten kilos in a couple of weeks. For the most part, gaining weight had gone quicker, since I hardly ever ate back then. When I did eat, my body absorbed everything that I put in it. Weight-loss on the other hand was almost always about me not eating at all and about the alcohol and other drugs dehydrating and constantly exhausting my body's reserves because it had to battle to break down those poisons.

In this new, sober life, eating was very difficult to navigate a sound path into. With a healthy diet, I would be able to keep the weight I was comfortable with. I knew that I couldn't exercise to get rid of my extra kilos – I really had only one option here, and that was to eat a balanced diet.

I had learned that it was alright to eat lots of eggs and this became an important platform. The high level of nourishment that eggs contain helped me when I was feeling low from being hungry. This resulted in my always having ready-boiled eggs in a container in the fridge. My therapist from the treatment centre had been taught this at a twelve-step program for sugar addiction. Without exaggeration, I can honestly say that eggs became one of my lifelines.

As a recovering person, I was oversensitive to being hungry. I noticed that I easily became alarmingly dizzy and weak from it – both physically, emotionally and mentally. When I took the last pre-boiled eggs out of the fridge, I always put a new pan on immediately. That way I was able to get nourishment quickly if I needed to. I often ate an egg while I was cooking, just to ease the hunger symptoms.

When Emma moved back home, I had gotten a small head start at a routine for putting together healthy, simple and tasty dishes. A lot of protein and just enough carbs, lots of greens and different kinds of sauces. This sounds easy enough, but it wasn't for me. There was always food in the freezer but somehow I kept forgetting to walk those three steps over from the worktop to get something out for the next day's supper. I wanted to let it defrost slowly in the fridge for the sake of the taste and quality of the meat (I was against owning and using a microwave in those days). At best, I got it right four out of seven days a week.

Every meal was difficult except for breakfast and I talked about this at all the places I had for talking. I couldn't understand this difficulty since I did enjoy eating. The aversion was tied to everything concerning the preparation. To barbecue and to go to a restaurant were wonderful luxuries when I just relaxed and enjoyed the food, but I cooked at home most days, and to get any meal ready was always madly exhausting.

At the hospital, my therapist informed me that almost all her recovering patients had problems with putting food on the table. She also pointed out that not only people with my background found this area to be a huge feat. To get the proper variation, to make everyone in the household happy, to serve wholesome meals and all this before you ran out of steam was really difficult.

I told her of how it looked in my head when I pictured a normal family routine, on a normal weekday afternoon:

One of the adults stood by the stove, maybe humming a popular tune while chopping vegetables and stirring the pans, cooking food that was magically and effortlessly picked out from the roomy yet well-stocked fridge. The other adult did a little non-disturbing tour of the home with the hoover, while the children chirped along about their day at school, happily setting the table and being generally useful and content. Later, when everyone was sitting down at the table, which brimmed with appetizingly overflowing bowls and pitchers, the whole family conversed joyously, all of them beaming, talking to each other and listening to each other's stories of their wonderful day and their dreams for the future.

She just stared at me, shaking her head.

"You do have fantasies don't you!?" She lost it laughing. "From which of the Hollywood movies was this taken, then?" Then she laughed at me, again.

"We had micro-wave dinners yesterday. Apart. And I didn't talk to my kids until late. They were confined to their rooms after having been unruly for days. My husband watched sports and mostly grumbled at me from the couch when I walked by. That's a normal family for you!" She cracked up again. Vast reaches of cluelessness.

If there was ever a turning point, it came there. I realised that this unmanageability and aversion to cooking and everything that goes with it was something I had to live with. No one was on top of things when they came home from work or after a day at the beach.

Knowing that most families struggle with meals at some point has helped me take the edge off my sense of being completely useless in the kitchen. Also the fact that I notice that I have evolved into being able to cook pretty tasty meals without too much effort in the last few years.

I asked for further hints at the Children and Family Unit (CaF) at the borough council. The counsellor asked what we used to eat in a week. I told her: minced meat, fish, chicken, meatballs and vegetarian dishes. She then told me to put together seven types of meals which Emma and I would plan for the weekdays together. This worked a few times and then this has been something I've gone back to doing on and off through the years.

As always, my strange disorder keeps me in a struggling, suffering mode until I remember to ask for help. Then I finally come to terms with accepting things as they are and make the necessary changes to get me out of various bottomless pits of agony. Breaching barriers of resistance to do good things for myself. Strange is the perfect word for this repeated behaviour that surfaces in very different areas in life. It's like I'm walking for miles on end with a sharp pebble in my shoe, hurting and limping until I suddenly acknowledge the pain and finally do something about it.

When I became clean, I truly believed that every dish had to be complete with meat, potatoes, sauce, salad and served with healthy beverages. I fretted for ages over whether I should have desserts every day, every other day or twice a week. The journey up to this day, when I can serve meals without too much thought and without living in constant desperation over what to serve, has been a long one. The worry is still there now and then but not nearly on the same scale as in the early days. Becoming a culinary guru is not on my list of ambitions. Serving what I regard as a healthy and fresh diet without the harsh and piquant seasoning of anguish is something I can say I've achieved. I would give that at least full marks in the Micheline Guide!

Exercise. I tried group aerobics. Catastrophe! The people in the ring all turned to the right while I lifted one arm and assuredly started walking towards the middle. They stood in a straight line and wiggled their toes while I continued doing knee lifts with loud grunts. Hopping on alternate feet whilst waving the opposite arm was a stop-right-now-or-you'll-hurt-someone-exercise. This was not for me.

I tried aqua aerobics. Not as bad, but this was mostly due to only being visible from the chin up.

No, solo gym visits with silent, unbreakable machines - that became my tune. My twelve-step sponsor worked as a gym instructor at this time and she showed me how to use the equipment. In 2008, I became friends with the monotony of the cross-trainer mixed with the pulling and pushing of levers of different types. Very easy and since everyone else doing this kind of training seems as self-centred as myself it suits me perfectly. I don't build muscles but I keep to an even work-out that takes 25 to 35 minutes to complete.

I needed to come to a decision about keeping to such a short interval workout because I hoped to keep this up in the long term. My goal was to work out two to three times a week. This was a good idea. I have been able to be a regular at the gym, except when something has come up that has made training impossible. Then I have usually been able to use my bicycle as an exercise tool as well as a means of transport. Biking along the sea-front and through the beautiful town of Malmö is inspiring for both mind and body.

I have noticed that I feel much better when I exercise regularly. It gets my body's own chemicals flowing, which clears my mind. My physical well-being is also noticeably improved by keeping to this routine. As with all things that are good for me, I need to be aware that I have to make an extra effort to get moving. Sometimes, an inspired feeling arises before I set off to the gym, but more often than not I need to kick myself off the sofa and inspiration doesn't come until I'm in the locker room. Sometimes I have to get a little way into my program, or to the end of it, before the sensation of satisfaction reaches my core. When this aversion attempts to rule me I need to know, to remind myself, that the feeling of satisfaction and fulfilment will come if I just do my exercises. Then it's all about simply shutting off the brain which keeps nagging at me to stay at home.

Sometimes, when the voice tells me to shorten the workout, I have a particularly potent motivational speech that I use to drown the urge to go to the showers:

"Hey! Do you remember those last minutes before the liquor store opened up in the morning, when the time couldn't pass fast enough?! Now you'd better just stay on this machine and take a couple of minutes to think about what you have today!"

That speech hasn't failed me yet. Undeniably inspirational and always making me stay for the full workout, no questions asked.

With my meals getting more regular and healthier, losing the remaining kilos happened slowly but surely. I also made other changes. From four to zero sugar lumps in my coffee and tea, from several to no sodas per week, and I tried to keep the candy and ice-cream parties for weekends only. Sometimes I even had to throw out old snacks and other sugar-bombs. It took me two and a half years to reach my comfortable weight and then I had lost the 25 kilos.

Smoking. When I reached four and a half years of sobriety, I had kept this weight steady for two years. Then the time came to stop smoking. I smoked five to ten home-rolled cigarettes daily and for the past year I'd had to use an asthma inhaler because I experienced trouble getting enough air. I even did a COPD test that year but it showed that I had better lung capacity than normal for female smokers my age. Thankfully.

What brought me to a turning point, of course, was finding myself on the brink of catastrophe – in June, I began getting radiating chest pains. Also, my grotesque cough got worse and people stared at me wherever I went.

The need for the inhaler seemed more and more absurd and the chest pains scared me senseless, but I still kept on smoking.

It was almost the same as it had been with the alcohol towards the end. The thought of Emma losing her sole present parent didn't motivate me. Neither did my own possible death. I churned these thoughts in my head and kept on smoking. One evening, I stood on the pavement in the middle of town and just cried. I was so frightened. And then I lit another cigarette.

When I came home that evening, I desperately searched inside for something that could inspire me. The fear was burning inside.

First, I came up with money. I cared about money. The second thing that hit me was looks. I cared about looks. I knew that the skin aged faster from smoking. It angered me that I couldn't find my rock bottom for Emma's or my own sake, but as the saying goes – rubble roads are better than no roads at all, so the embarrassing truth was that two of the deadly sins carried me through my first weeks, well, months, of being a non-smoker. Vanity and greed.

The first week I was angry and barked at everyone and everything that had anything to do with smoking and, also, anything that had nothing to do with smoking.

"Bloody, f-ed up idiocy! I can't smoke!"

"Gnnn. I hate this! This truly, truly sucks!" "Spoiled bastards who can smoke!" and so on and so forth on the same theme.

In between these frequent outbursts, I fed myself with thoughts that I had saved 70 Euros on the monthly budget, that I was slowing the invasion of wrinkles on my face and slowly more profound values began to weave themselves into my consciousness. The heightened life quality, staying alive and being among the more-sane.

A tip that I had hung on to, when the all but deafening urge to solve life's problems through lighting up again bombarded me, was that the want for a cigarette only appeared as an alarming need for seven to twenty seconds at a time. If I pulled through those short attacks without taking the decision to go out and buy tobacco, the crazy urge would disappear. It worked only because I fought as hard as I could. The desire to stop didn't come of its own accord – I didn't suddenly realise the beauty of being smoke-free. This was a struggle and the urge still washes over me at times. The lie of the Marlboro-man, the handsome, composed horse-owner beaming with health, lighting up and becoming one with the glorious sunrise.

The anger simmered. For longer and longer periods of time I was able to think of other things than smoking. The truth of the bizarre notion to inhale numerous, unchartered poisons, other than the nicotine, into the fine tissue of my sensitive and miraculous lungs by inhaling hot smoke began to touch the strings of truth within and at more frequent intervals than the urge to relapse.

I used a milder form of nicotine for a year afterwards but with very calculated restraint. It was something I stopped using completely a year later, all according to my plan.

As it had been with the other drugs, I knew that I would only start smoking again if I gave in to the notion that my life would be more fabulous if I took to the nicotine again. The urge to smoke can't kill me but the cigarettes definitely can.

After I had stopped smoking, I caught a strange virus. At the same time I had just agreed to be a test person for a large ice-cream company. Struggling with waves of high fever for a couple of months, I had to stop exercising and sitting at home with a freezer literally filled to the brim with luxuriously delicious ice-cream. My new pacifier was a given. Within two months, I gained ten kilos. I lost all my self-control and developed an addiction to sugar that I had never experienced before and that I still need to be observant of. It took a year to regain my comfortable weight and it was so hard that I really was close at giving up sometimes.

Now I feel that I have found a balance that I can handle. I am not skinny and I am not a work-out-oholic. I do make sure that I take care of myself in a loving manner. When I met the man of my life in 2011 I gained a few kilos when we just sat there on the sofa beaming at each other for quite a few months, but then I was restored to sanity and came back to healthy habits again.

Much blood, sweat and tears have been shed in getting to and then keeping on this constructive way of life. To be healthy and loving towards my body is not something that comes to me in a spontaneous and joyful impulse, but I find hope and comfort in knowing that I'm not alone with having to walk that extra mile, or two, to keep my body happy. The most important carrot is that I keep reminding myself of the difference between how I feel with and without what I regard as healthy habits. The difference between doing and not doing is so great that I get my act together and do something good for my body on a daily basis. Mostly, anyhow.

My years in the real world since I became sober in 2006 are a gift. I live on bonus time. The destructiveness that always carried the winning cup in my earlier years has to bow down to this woman who strides along with a hunger for life and a burning flame for co-existing. My gratitude and hope toward my ongoing recovery is something I cherish – and it helps me do good things for myself. My desire is to live a life where health and feeling good take a well-earned place in the foreground.

Parenting

I have a child, a wonderful girl, who came into this world in the late summer of 2001. She lived with me for a little more than the first four years of her life, but I was available to her only from early spring, 2006. She was then four and a half years old.

This is an awful truth. I had been utterly incapable of taking care of myself then and, even less, of being responsible for another person. Every evening I had lain down beside her, listening to her breathing silently, and every night I had silently asked her forgiveness for having put her through yet another day in the shadow of alcohol.

In the silence that emerges in the moment before sleep, thoughts took me of how the next day would be different, soothing me to sleep. The next day, I acted on the same worn-out agenda and my actions were repetitions of the same patterns that my little girl had been born into.

Day in and day out, my intoxication was the only light I could see to carry me through another day's routine. The glorified sips that were in truth fuelling only darkness on the ever more rickety and worn-down treadmill of our lives.

Emma was taken care of by the municipality in November of 2005. During that year we had been at a treatment centre for mothers with addiction and their children. Twice. Despite this effort from the social welfare authorities to help me find my way to leading a new way of life, I kept on using alcohol.

I saw how Emma became more and more apathetic after we came home from the treatment centre the last time. My thoughts spun about, I couldn't manage parenthood since I didn't have any desire to stop my abuse. I couldn't stand hurting my beautiful girl this way anymore. Among the very few good things I did that year was to let my daughter move into an environment where adults who were able to see to her needs took care of her for me. She went to live at the city orphanage.

I was allowed to come to be with her at the orphanage four times a week. After these three-hour visits, as always, I went straight to the mirage of relief - the liquorstore. In the end, though, I couldn't cope with this awful non-existence anymore. It was only me and the bottles and I was done.

Emma had lived at the orphanage for four months when I finally found my way out. I hardly understood what was going on during those first, confused days of sobriety but when I visited Emma one time, about a week later, she peered at me quizzically for a moment, and then matter-of-factly stated:

"Mother, you have become well. Now I can move back home!"

The truth of her words hit me with full force and her clear-minded observation woke me to the world in which I was now, apparently, taking part. From her having hardly ever mentioned my addiction in her whole life, to her drawing such a sensible and insightful conclusion gave me a rude awakening to how harshly affected she had actually been.

The saying that "drunks tell the truth" will never be believed in our home. We know how the truth hides behind that platitude – the children suffer in silence while the drunkards babble, all the while calculating how to attain the next sip in "peace".

I actively search for and partake in all guidance I can find when it comes to being a parent - I certainly need to. I regularly come to a point where I can see that I lack the ability to guide my child. When I was little, we had very sweet nannies who lived with us, but they were teenagers and very busy at being young. My references for being an adult come from Hollywood and Disney ideals. To admit that I don't have the first clue about living in a sound family is actually my strength. I am an unwritten page that I can fill with what seems to work in the different phases of her young years.

As with most things, being a parent is something I need to be humble towards. My impulses usher me towards acting to fulfil my own needs, turning a blind eye to Emma's. The only solution seems to be that I keep a constant awareness of reviewing my choices. This includes talking to others about what I do and don't do in our little family unit.

I also realise that some of the difficulties I encounter are dysfunctional parenting patterns which I've inherited from the generations before me. I am passing down these behaviours to Emma. This is something I take very seriously. Besides seeking help for my development as a parent within the healthcare and welfare systems, I also go to a twelve-step organisation that focuses on the issues of being a child from a dysfunctional family. I get hope from seeing others going from unmanageable lives to being able to act differently.

Often I can be overwhelmed by a sensation of never, ever being able to change or pass on anything remotely healthy to my little girl, but that is not true. When I work for it, change is already happening. A new way of life can be our reality despite there having been innumerable generations of social inadequacy before us. I don't have to be a failure as a parent.

When I feel the need for it, I can get counselling from the Children and Family Unit (CaF) within our borough. I bring up my shortcomings and get another perspective when I see my therapist. I talk to my fiancé and get feedback, whether I like it or not. I also talk and listen to other parents and my friends. I focus when this topic is raised at any of the organisations I visit, especially at the twelve-step meetings. And Hollywood and Disney still do their bit to inspire me.

I do everything I can to be as good a parent as I can. I also need to back off a lot. Sometimes I've almost been smothering the poor girl. Most importantly, I have to act on the things I feel might benefit our family and then time will tell.

This can sound as if I'm on the verge of graduating as the all-time solid guru of flawless parenting, but I'm very sorry to disappoint. Whenever I think I've gotten the hang of it and all the bats in the belfry seem to be hanging according to the proper seating arrangement, then it all just goes scarily, completely off any map I thought I knew how to read. Then Emma, or I, have apparently embarked upon a new phase of emotional or social challenge. Unforeseeable events occur or life just has a whole bunch of things happen that no one, or any knowledge in the world, can prevent from happening.

In Skåne, my province in Sweden, there is a saying that says it all:

"Oh, well, hello! Are you surprised much?"

When I'm there, not knowing anything about anything, I spontaneously enter a new phase of desperation, using wild gestures combined with nagging, without blanks and completely without a second thought. That is the reality inside the walls of our loving home. That's why I often pray for help in keeping my mind as open as possible. I do believe though, that my willingness to be a good parent is winning more than half of this battle. If nothing else, my daughter feels in her heart that this nagging, worrying, crazy person loves her, regardless of my better and my better and my worse sides.

If I hadn't looked for solutions outside our family and considered new ways to tackle parenting the last time such an evolutionary mutation hit us, I wouldn't be sitting here writing this book, or the last one for that matter. I've noticed that following my own mind's impulses is not the optimal way to go about things. When difficult challenges arise, my inclination to flee pops up like a Jack-in-the-Box, smiling and nodding with believable allure. My saviours are, as always, hope, trust and thankfulness. These spiritual guides keep me in the here and now and I remind myself that this life will never ever get boring.

Through the social welfare system, I was able to take part in a parenting course called "The Incredible Years", which is an internationally-renowned program. On this course, I was informed of many tools I could use on a daily basis and, in between every class, we got a whole week to perform different exercises at home with our kids.

The exercises could concern boundaries, encouragement, praise and exploring how we could play best together. I felt very comfortable with trying these methods out at home, up until the week when we were told to give ourselves praise in front of our children. This sounded fine when they described it to me. The meaning of this was to inspire the child to develop a natural, normal feeling, that it is alright to have a positive image of oneself.

When we came home I thought I would get right to it, but no words would come out. Instead, I got an awkward feeling in my gut, shoving aside the plan of doing the exercise that day. The next day, the same queasy feeling erupted. Now I got angry.

I was so proud of all the things I had accomplished in the past year. I sat writing long lists of things I was grateful for and all the things I had that were both nice and healthy every day. Now I couldn't say a single word of praise about myself out loud to strengthen the person I loved the most in this world! I saw that there was something very, very wrong with this picture. Somehow I had to make this work!

I searched for the right words and the right moment all day, but the sincerity I looked for didn't surface. I decided that I would have to force myself. After dinner,

Emma stayed at the kitchen table and I stood with my back turned to her doing the dishes as usual and then I got it! Out of nowhere, I suddenly spoke, forcing the words out of my mouth:

"I am so very efficient to be doing the dishes straight after the meal today!"

Luckily Emma didn't see the awkward face I made. She didn't respond either. I always did the dishes after meals and maybe that was why she was so quiet. It was strange that she didn't say anything – we always talked lots about everything and anything. She must have felt my unease.

I kept forcing myself to do this exercise for the next few days despite the obnoxious distaste it awoke inside me. My repertoire with self-appraising phrases expanded with time and reached unexpected heights:

"I am so proud! Before picking you up at the day-care today I posted a letter that I've been putting off for ages!"

"I am really good at arriving on time for my appointments!"

"I was brave as anything today! I went to a gym for the first time!"

"I'm so happy! This morning I dared call a friend that I really like and we decided to go for coffee later in the week!"

It became easier to say these things every time and after a while I even began talking like that when my friends were with us. Eventually Emma didn't even have to be with me when I did. I have kept up doing this until this day and, even though the feeling of awkwardness still arises from time to time, the words often come straight from the heart and that gladdens me.

What this exercise has meant to Emma becomes very apparent when she talks about herself with other people. Only six months after I had arm-twisted the first affirmation out of myself, when Emma was eight years old, we sat in her classroom discussing her evaluation for that term with the teacher. When the teacher had gone through the different subjects, she asked Emma what thoughts she had about her achievements.

"We-ell, I 'm really good at maths," her whole face shone with unclouded pride and certainty, "and then I do very well at everything else as well, except spelling. I really need to work on that," she said, nodding with an expression of sincere reflection.

I was dumbfounded. I had never in my entire life had such insightful self-esteem as this young lady. Spontaneously, I kissed her forehead and she wriggled happily, winked at me and then kept on the conversation as if everything was quite normal – which this situation apparently was for her.

I gave myself a big pat on the back for showing my daughter a tool to use to be able to view herself with self-love and self-worth. Thinking about what could have happened if I had skipped that week's exercise scares me a little. It has become such an important foundation for her development and sense of belonging in this world. Also the self-affirmation process affected me so profoundly that my behaviour and self-esteem was heightened which, of course, has also caught on with Emma as an acceptable way to view oneself.

Participating in this course prepared me well. It was perfect to attend at such an early stage, right at the start of creating our family-structure. I am thankful for every second the two leaders put into guiding us.

I have put those different tips and tricks to good use up to this day - even to guide the teenager she became in 2014. They told us that to treat a teenager like a newborn was the most valuable thing to remember when the "hormone-poisoning" of puberty set in. Comfort her when she yells - but in the teens the shouting is sometimes with words I just have to be deaf to. To see to it that she sleeps, eats, gets fresh air and exercise. I also need to let her show her feelings and I am doing a lot of listening to my teenagers thoughts and theories, trying to keep in mind to not always express my own reflections.

Not having any healthy references to a teenage period myself, I took this advice to heart and I've put it to good use ever since that unpredictable person suddenly took over my sweet little girl's room. Emma is growing up.

It is a wondrous journey to be a parent. Never a dull moment!

The CaF have always been there for us as soon as I've had questions or if Emma has needed someone to talk to. When she was seven-and-a-half years old, she was enrolled in a group that focused on children who had grown up with one or more parents with some kind of emotional disorder. The children were of the same age but their backgrounds were very diverse.

Emma's parent was a recovering addict but others had parents who still used drugs. There were those who had absent parents, there were children of gamblers, workaholics, some had witnessed violence and so on. Here, Emma was supposed to learn to identify what she was feeling and learn to recognise and express her needs. This was all opposed to what she had learned growing up, which was using her emotional tentacles to tip-toe around my emotional state. She had tried to use what she grasped from my behaviour to understand what I "needed". During her first four and a half years, my prioritising getting alcohol into my system had been what she learned to be an important part of our lives.

One goal of this group was for the children to learn how to lift the burden of "attention" which had been forced upon them. The guilt that came with never being able to be the one who made the parent happy. Another goal was to learn how to manage and allow feelings to be felt. A third was to let the child know that there were others out there who were like themselves – that their neglected childhood was something that others had suffered too.

Emma took these goals to heart. I noticed a strong and healthy development in her spontaneity and emotional balance. Also, maybe the most important thing is that she has become more and more able to give voice to when she is in need of attention and when something upsets her. She is also able to ask for advice and make responsible choices on her path to adulthood.

The children there also made a solemn promise never to tell the other children's stories to anyone outside the group and Emma kept that oath very responsibly and with great pride. This nourished the children's integrity, which was something none of them had been brought up to cherish.

We, the parents, are still very much in the dark about what they talked about in there, but the positive outcome seen in our children's behaviour was so apparent that this confidentiality was easily accepted.

Emma told me about their activities though. They drew on themes important to them, listened to each other in group settings and the leaders read different stories that were filled with symbolism about the things they had to identify.

There was a meditation exercise that she still uses to this day. It was of a mountain that she was to climb. On her walk, she met different people that were of significance to her. When she finally reached the top, she was alone and there stood a tree onto which she could string feelings of her choosing. She describes this meditation giving her a strong sense of serenity. It makes me so happy that she has found this in her life.

For my child, these sessions became an oasis that she looked forward to every week and I had to live with being curious about what she talked about in there. There was no doubting the value of the things she gained by attending. It was my responsibility to let her develop a strong sense of self.

A trait I have learned to see as an advantage in my parenting is that I let other grown-ups, and especially trained professionals, guide her in her development. The spontaneous idea that I "ought to manage this by myself" has proven to be a selfish lie that my brain tries, time and time again, to pass off as the truth. I have had to surpass the feelings of shame, insufficiency and vain pride and look at the benefits Emma shows by having other adults in her life. Then all my doubts evaporate.

Once, when Emma was nine, I asked the CaF for another kind of therapeutic support. It concerned her awkward relationship with her biological father, whom she had only met a few times since she was two-and-a-half years old. At nine, she was at that age when existential questions begin to surface. She knew that addiction is a deadly disease and so she knew that her father, who still used alcohol back then, was endangering his life on a daily basis.

This was a hot potato for me. I found it very difficult to be objective. I was torn between many emotions when these questions arose that were causing her so much pain. This was something that Emma, being very sensitive to my emotions, picked up on so I decided that we had to get outside help.

The social worker I talked to at the CaF told me that Emma was too young to have private talks with a professional, but that we could set it up so that I could attend but where Emma would be the one doing the talking. Other appointments would be set for me with parental coaching and feedback from the therapist to see if I could get better at being supportive and a listener at home.

This request was brought before a board for approval. When I found that we had gotten the go ahead, I called the woman who would be holding these sessions with us.

"Maybe I'm exaggerating. Are we taking up space and time from people who need your support more than us?"

This question had been oozing at the back of my mind for a while now. Emma had grown into a very direct and anchored person and was harmonious for the most part. She often laughed in her sleep which proved to me that, deep down, she was quite content.

The answer I got came instantly:

"Oh no, you don't! That is not the way you should be thinking. There are so many who would need this type of support, but they don't ask for it. They don't search out the possibilities to strengthen their children. Emma and you are absolutely worthy of this. And after the nightmares you've lived through – don't you doubt it! Thanks to your asking for help, you are building a family based on strong foundations. Your lives have turned around in this way only because you are searching out solutions!"

She helped me see this in another light. Looking at my spontaneous reaction of being unworthy showed me how difficult it is to ask for help. This occasion serves as a reminder to think twice when I'm drawn to managing without other people. I believe that many parents and other people can relate to feeling fear when facing one's own inadequacy. As if it makes me vulnerable to admit this to someone else. The gratitude for all the support we have been given overtakes any lingering doubts. It is important to receive input about how to raise my child and also to follow my gut feeling about the advice given.

We have talked about Emma's homework, her school, my crazy urges to always do things, or rather, do lots of things, questions about food and how she can have time for friends outside school.

In my private talks, we have looked at my role as a stable and safe haven for Emma in her daily routines. I easily move into drama and catastrophic thinking and have gotten well-needed feedback on what she can actually manage on her own and when she needs supportive parenting. I try to let her struggle without losing my cool.

These talks have touched on varying subjects for the both of us and often others than we had initially asked for. It is always an inspiring and enriching experience to share with someone outside the family. This has also resulted in personal growth that extends into life as a whole and relationships beyond our little family.

There is a lot to keeping a family together but not as much as I tend to blow it up to be. Thankfully, I have been told that many parents do what I do – worry too much. Maybe that's a parent's job.

To know that I have the same concerns as many other mothers and fathers helps me keep my feet on the ground. I am an ambitious parent and there are many more like me out there. I try to keep a calm outlook, which is well-needed during these times of teenage roller-coaster surprises.

As they were in the wake of the parenting course, these therapeutic appointments have enriched me as much as they have Emma, if not more. The overwhelming bits of being a single parent have become less scary and sometimes I even ease into a comfortable role. Still learning every day, sometimes the bats start rioting and I go wild, but at least I am better at seeing when this happens and can turn the spotlights down a notch. Luckily, because as Emma said a while back:

"Mother, it's a child's job to see to giving their parents lots to worry about! It says so in the children's manual on page 43!" Then she laughed out loud at my flabbergasted face.

The truth in her words run deep, though – who else is she going to test her wings on?

I talked a lot to my therapist at the hospital. My addictive recovery has been best taken care of at my self-help meetings, but at the hospital I have discussed and been given feedback at length about what could be considered "normal" parenting and what can be related to my disorder. Through the years at the ward, I've only had therapists who themselves had children. Since being a parent is a large part of my life, this has come up a lot. My need to defuse and normalise is always a current process for me.

My latest counsellor gave me some advice that I've put to good use at home. My daughter takes after me and has a dramatic flair that bursts out sometimes when she retells things that have happened. On one occasion it was about a situation that had played out in her class involving her. I got caught up in the drama and reacted very emotionally. Afterwards, I noticed that Emma had in no way been helped by my reaction and I had only lost lots of energy. My wise counsellor tilted her head and said the most ingenious thing I had heard in ages:

"You can just say that this is a typical thing to do at her age."

I furrowed my eyebrows at this.

"What do you mean?"

"Well, just say 'That is so typical of a nine-year-old.' Or you can just give a shrug and shake your head like a wise old lady and say "Well that is such a typical thing to happen to a nine-year-old. You acted exactly your age!" Because when she gets to hear something like that, it will help her let go of her frustrated feelings about the situation. When she hears that her reaction is perfectly normal, it will make it easier for her to look at what happened with an open mind."

I used it the other day when it was in regard to a reaction to a teacher at her school:

"Well that's exactly what a teenager would do. You'll pull through. You'll see."

It always feels so nonsensical to say it like that and I don't understand how it works but that doesn't matter when I always see her calming down and moving on.

There are so many examples of how these behaviourists have supported me through periods when I've stood helpless before my role as a parent and wondered how I should react to what she is going through. They have offered new angles and objective observations on Emma's but, more importantly, on my reactions. I will always know that I can reach out for advice whenever the need arises.

Talking to parents in other contexts has been very important. Listening when others share at my self-help meetings about how they have handled their parenting when it comes up has been helpful as well. This has become an essential, natural and ongoing part of managing. I need to hear from those who have first-hand, practical and what I would define as evidence-based knowledge of recovery. To have the opportunity to be inspired by the solutions that have worked for them as adults as well as being parents. It is a gift to listen to people who remain in sobriety with a desire to stay that way over a lifelong period of time. I often find something that I can relate to and even try at home. If nothing else I get a spark to keep on searching for a way that works for us in the situation we are in at the moment.

To be a parent in recovery has this positive side-effect – I get to listen and learn in a setting where deep truths, both the positive ones and the failures, are shared freely. This helps me immensely in getting perspective on being a parent among other parents as a whole, addicts or not. It has been an advantage to have admitted my powerlessness, because this has meant that I actually listen to others – something I never did before. I get the power and the tips and tricks to get to be an evolving adult.

These true tales of excursions into the unmapped terrain of parenthood from other parents' home situations give me the courage to approach this part of my life. It tickles my practical sense to make changes and dare trying new things without backing down in front of the fear of failure. Hollywood and Disney are still beautiful and idealistic utopias to me but to make such happy sparkling rainbows real I need proper and sturdy tools that work in real life.

As time goes by, I constantly see that Emma is getting through her tunnels of obstacles and coming out on the other side a bit wiser, and all this despite my brain's doomsday scenarios and dramatic outbursts. My worry doesn't pass – it only goes from one area to the next. This is apparently my lot as a parent just as it is to the lot of all of us who are doing this wonderful thing.

Guiding a child is mostly done whilst caught up in the jungle of troubled concern!

The little one has become a teenager. When she was twelve, I was at a meeting for parents with the class mentors at her school and I brought up the subject of alcohol. The counsellor was there and he was eager to test his recently-gathered knowledge from a course he'd attended on the subject. I thought it was important to talk about this issue but I didn't know how the other parents would react. Most teenagers in Sweden have their alcohol debut in their fourteenth to sixteenth year, even though it isn't legal to use before you turn eighteen. Despite this, most grown-ups had their first wine or beer at this early age, which might make it feel difficult to put forward a firm boundary for your teenager.

I was very nervous and feared that I would be viewed as the smart aleck of the group. I was happily surprised by the positive response we got. The goals were to inform our kids about the effects that alcohol has on the body. To elaborate on the positive effects abstinence would have on a young person's ability to develop social and mental skills without the crutch of a drug. To be firm and clear about the age-limit of using alcohol legally.

Most of us hadn't let social skills be weaved into our personalities without alcohol. Most could relate to having danced with a partner under the influence at our very first disco for example. With my new eyes I can see that sobriety is an enormously enriching quality from a personal development point of view and this is a personal growth that I want to allow my child to experience. I can imagine the strength of self a sober young mind will generate. A priceless route toward establishing a young person's self-worth. I have the responsibility to hand Emma this alternative which will benefit her inner growth.

She plays musical instruments and when she was five years old she joined a theatre group which she still goes to. Offering her these alternative interests will hopefully make it easier for her to choose healthy leisure-time activities during the young adult years. Something less dangerous than drug binging. I'm wishing it will save me from having to enforce harsh rules, evade terrible rows and spare us from unfathomable worries.

Alcohol and nicotine are prohibited for everyone under the age of eighteen in our family and the consequences will be notable if she breaks those rules. Telephone and computer withdrawal, allowances held back and curfews. Drugs of any kind are not an option for a child under our roof!

After eighteen, she will choose her own path. By then I hope she will be so well-informed that her choices will be healthy ones.

It is a miraculous journey I have been priviledged to share with Emma. Our life together was so close to ending in November 2005. I never thought I would be able to stop using alcohol and my doctor had told me that I was in a life-threatening physical shape. Once again, I have to thank the anonymous person that called the police when I was out on the town drunk with my little 2-year-old girl and which led to my getting to go to the treatment centre. The gift of our little family has grown from that seed of compassion! Thank you!

I was shown that there were others like me out there. People who had found a way to live without the urge to be intoxicated. I am doing my best to be responsible and I am often taken aback at how this actually is our reality today.

We are in the midst of creating a new family constellation with my fiancé, Emma's bonus dad, and I'm not parenting alone anymore. Since September 2011 when he asked me/us out for the first time. I had stood watching him tie his shoes after a social call at our place. He stayed, fidgeting for quite a while in our hallway. I remember thinking: "If he doesn't ask me out now I'll call him and ask him to go for a coffee with me later this week..." Then he suddenly said, staring at his sneakers:

"Have you seen The Smurfs in 3D?"

I just blanked and answered:

"E-eeeh, no, not really. Have you?" A smile shone inside me as well as on my face. I realised instantly that he included Emma when he, in his own charming way, asked me out for a date.

There our new family unit began moulding itself and today it is as if we, all three, are made for each other.

Emma and Per have created their own secret society to discuss the mothers of this world and have created a relationship where I am no longer needed. To just sit and watch them talking, snorkelling, watching TV and even arguing is totally, incredibly wonderful.

Having a life partner, having someone to share the responsibilities of parenting with and who loves his bonus daughter unconditionally, fills me with gratitude beyond words.

Thoughts of the wonderful day when we will eventually move in together warms me. I will probably give in to their endless nagging soon...

With love for humanity in the foreground I believe that everything is possible. I hope Emma will mature with a sense of responsibility towards life and a longing to take care of the endless possibilities that lie at our feet on this miraculous planet of ours.

She sometimes expresses sadness about how we plunder our world's finite resources for shortsighted profits. It hurts me to see her suffer with compassion. I then answer her that all I can do to bear that same pain is to change my own self and do things differently wherever I possibly can.

To plant seeds of love, hope and faith.

To set boundaries for unacceptable behaviour.

To show her that to actually change is all about doing

something differently rather than repeating the same destructive patterns of passive theorising, disliking of others and spoiling things.

These are my goals as a parent.

My desire is to be able to keep supporting her towards adulthood so that she hopefully can embark on her days as a grown-up with a life that inspires her, and the people around her, to make good choices.

Occupation

I wanted to. As surprising to observe as my desire to stop using drugs had been to me, so was this sudden longing to be like most other people. A desire was born to get an education and to eventually have a job. This motivation, to create a working career, germinated from my new sense of belonging and I sprang into action.

When I was five years old, I dreamt of being an author when I grew up. Then the years went by and I lived with that dream constantly nagging at me. What I grew up to be was something completely different. I became a person who was insanely focused on always having access to alcohol and, periodically, other drugs.

Being intoxicated altered my mind and what I wrote under the influence didn't feel true.

I had held down temporary jobs sparsely through the years, but towards the end I didn't work at all. I didn't even attempt any criminal endeavours during those last years of addiction. What energy surges I had were spent on never being empty-handed, keeping the acquisition of more drugs running smoothly.

Earlier in life it had been different though.

My drug of choice was always alcohol but I took a break from this drug after having overdosed when I was fifteen.

Soon after that, I tried hash for the first time. Because I was a minor I was already used to having to sneak about with the alcohol, but with cannabis I was now on a track that was beyond most grown-ups, and definitely beyond the law. To justify my use of an illegal intoxicant, I created norms that lay outside the ones of society.

I was often together with friends who also used alcohol and other pacifying drugs. We followed in the footsteps of addicts and criminals from generations before us. We listened to those who were more experienced in this area and we created rules that fit our gang. We redefined everything that stood in our way so that we had airtight arguments to justify keeping on using and dealing.

The most revolutionary and harmful justifications were the ones I used on myself. I had to modify reality to suit me, creating explanations for the circumstances of my life. The reasons I saw that made my addiction so special, which the surrounding world was too ignorant and begrudging to understand. They only wanted to hinder me, I thought.

In the back of my mind, the truth beckoned to be heard. One eighth of a beat behind that voice of con-science, I fervently wrote the most ludicrous defences for being able to keep on following my destructive impulses. Working hard to mindlessly stay in pursuit of my buzz.

Inside, a small voice bickered at me concerning my health issues and what my true place on this Earth ought to be. Gnawing thoughts of the sorrow and worries my loved ones had about my situation were effectively stifled. I was only running on the impulse to use more drugs.

For 25 years, nothing new happened under my sun.

When I woke up from these hazy decades of stupor, I was 39 years of age and my view on living abruptly rotated 180 degrees. No one was more perplexed than I. Not only was the never-ending hunting over, but the longing for a legal, meaningful and productive occupation suddenly became a strong goal for me. I awoke from 25 years of ingenious refusal to take part, constantly weaving theories of the evil world and now, suddenly, I burned to be one of the threads in the cooperation of society.

A yearning rose in me to have a workplace on Earth.

I had shunned, vilified and belittled what I now coveted – the possibility of being employed. I began fulfilling the dream I had of being able to pitch in, to be a part of building and strengthening the world around me. I had many reasons for wanting this.

To support our little family. To be able to save money for going on adventures, experiencing miraculous wonders in the world. To afford to explore what kind of hobbies Emma and I would enjoy.

There were many things woven into getting a job.

Through a friend, I learned that there was an EU-project for women who had lived outside society, just like me. The project was called "Växa", which means "Grow".

Zero tolerance for any drugs, including alcohol and illegal addictive substances, was a requirement for those who wished to participate. That seemed to be the kind of safe environment I would fit into.

When I had been sober for two months I put in an application to attend Växa with the social services. Six months later, six eternal months later, I got confirmation of having been admitted onto the project. I started going there in the mornings for four hours, four days a week.

Slowly but surely, I was taught how to use the internet and I took lessons in Swedish, English and maths.

I was offered to be signed up for driving lessons. This was amazing because it was almost mandatory to have a driver's license in order to get any kind of job. I took that chance even though I couldn't begin taking those lessons at once. I was still in my first year of recovery and felt that I needed more time.

The most challenging part of this project were the classes in "life". The hours we spent learning about leading an ordinary, healthy lifestyle were incredibly useful and I was surprised when I noticed that I found these lessons the most challenging.

I was able to try different activities as a taster of what I might fill my everyday life with. As a motivated average Swede in the making, I stoically faced my fears.

I went on guided tours of Malmö city where we were told about the history and anecdotes of the different parks and their many sculptures. On our walks, we found out interesting facts about the buildings. I went to one of the borough's municipal offices, where a staff member informed us of what they could help us, the citizens, with as she pointed at us - a beaming crowd. We were shown how to use their free internet access, printers and the free phone one could use when calling the different administrations there, the social services and other departments within the city. We also met politicians who explained the work they did and how we could influence and make suggestions about how the town was run.

We also went to cultural establishments. The library was a place with which I had first-hand and regular experience, but many of the group had never been inside. I got the opportunity to watch several plays at different theatres, went to a beauty parlour, went to a gym induction and saw a movie at the cinema.

These visits punched great holes in the delusions I'd had through life about how "ordinary" people lived their lives in a grey, dreary world of monotony. To watch the people who weren't in our group naturally enjoying themselves, savouring their leisure time at these places, made a huge impression on me. There were a myriad of interesting and nice things to do in the world of the "normies". Activities that I had known of and, in many cases, had been taken to as a child, but never even considered doing myself.

Being able to sit in the much-frequented beauty parlour having the pedicure I had chosen, gave me insights into several aspects of life that lured me.

I was close to tears when my feet were pampered by the caring beautician's hands. My feet which had trampled too many cobblestones, taking me to too many awfully destructive places. The girl who performed the treatment was very young. Her manner showed great pride in her profession and chatting with her felt sincere and friendly. I caught myself hoping that I would be able to feel such contentment with whatever my occupational field would be.

Going on the tours of Malmö, I got to learn about workplaces that I had never given any thought to before. To get to learn the city's history and how it worked in today gave the town's people, both poor and rich, new depths. Adding to the importance of all these different occupations. So many people lived their lives building and caring for this city. It dawned on me how closed off my worldview had been. I, who had always expressed myself as a world connoisseur and who had truly believed I possessed an air of insightfulness.

Actually, I was the one who had existed in a grey, monotonous rut with my alcohol, day in and day out. Not the rest of the world.

As the paradox goes – the sorrow of having had such delusions became what fuelled my love to keep on exploring the world. Curiosity inspired me to aspire.

I didn't have a clue as to what I wanted to be when I grew up, but the more I saw of this new world and with every adventure I went on in this universe of new experiences, my desire to stay on the path expanded. I was often startled by a resounding thankfulness to be in the midst of a weekday routine and the taste for living a "normal life" was strengthened by the hour. To me this was as far from normal as anything I had ever experienced.

Commonplace things for most were often exciting and unknown to me. Routines, the social interaction at Växa and the most wonderful thing of all, finishing off a day, being on my way home to Emma and enjoying the satisfaction of having been useful, warmed my very core.

The contrast between this gratification compared to the fleeting and artificially-rewarding chemical rut I was used to with the alcohol was like night and day. The longer my addiction had held me in its grasp, the more shut off I had become to pure appreciation of the finer things in life.

To fill myself with these adventures and challenges

was true nourishment. I was in love with the desire to be a part of society and I enjoyed every moment.

Writing books was not something I considered to be a proper occupation. At least not for me. Other people could be authors but I couldn't wrap my mind around the idea that this could include me. I had only a little amateur experience. No schooling or even keyboard practice and I didn't have any ideas for a book, for that matter. But my storytelling flame was urgently burning with inextinguishable magma and didn't listen to reason. I made a deal with Katja, my English teacher, that I would be able to take a writer's course during the Swedish lessons.

I used a book called "Write from the heart: Unleashing the Power of Your Creativity" by Hal Zena Bennett. I followed the exercises outlined in this book, which were extremely rewarding for my writing process.

One day, Katja stopped me in the hallway and beckoned me aside.

"Lotten. I am not your friend and it would be a cheap trick to play on you if what I'm about to tell you wasn't true." She eyed me to see that I was following. "You are a very good writer. You should pursue this and enrol in any type of education you can that would develop this talent."

To mask the stab I felt in my gut, a sheepish smile instinctively spread over my face.

"Ehm. Oh. Well, yes, thank you very much. I'll really

think about that," I stammered while thinking "Not!" and her words met stone inside me.

An emotional cramp soared into every part of my being and I had to call in a babysitter to be able to go to an unplanned self-help meeting that evening. Disciplined but much uninspired writing followed for the next six months.

Thanks to having attended the parenting course and having done the exercise with the positive affirmations regarding my good qualities, I could observe myself and see what the problem was. So I just kept on following the course in Bennett's book, but the "writing from the heart" part felt very distant.

The time at Växa gave me a priceless platform to stand on for practicing summoning courage for venturing into the unknown. Something many people learn at a much earlier stage in life. Unfortunately, this project had to shut down when the funding period from the EU ended. This was a great loss for the city. If the town had continued funding it, many more women and their families would have benefitted.

Many of the participants from my group are doing very well up to this day. Through the years, I have noticed that the women who attended Växa made it in unusually high numbers. Many are still sober, many have jobs, others went on to education and several have reached the tops of ladders within various firms. The sunshine stories are many among these women. People who had almost been predestined to perish, destroying our bodies with death defying life-styles, aliens to society such as we were. Women whose talents never would have flowered without this special and enabling project leading us gently on to discover an inner desire for integration.

We were allowed an individually-set pace in a very tolerant environment. I am eternally grateful that there was an effort of this kind exactly when I became sober. I truly wish that others could get the same chance that we did.

The founders of Växa and my healthcare givers all talked to me about my sensitivity to stress, which in my ears sounded exaggerated. But, since the choices I had made for myself in my earlier life had only led me to life-threatening situations, I had made a decision to listen to and at least consider what others said to me.

There were four different people who, uninfluenced by the others, had all come to this same conclusion, so despite not relating to an ounce of what they were talking about, at least I listened. But listening didn't help me take it to heart. There wasn't even the weakest twinge of recognition within. I wanted to get on with my integration into the coalition of mankind. I was on fire!

Getting me to slow down was really hard. I had my

hands full with Emma, our home and hobbies and taking care of my recovery, which had to be number one or otherwise everything else would disintegrate. Then there was the food issue and exercise, of course. Well, alright then, I would ease off. A bit. Slow the pace and try to let time become my friend.

I noticed that it was difficult to make time for starting the process of getting my driver's license. I was promised that the driving lessons and the studies would be kept on ice for me even if I couldn't manage them during the period when I was at Växa. This helped me lower the demands I put on myself.

It wasn't easy to ease the pressure though. I wanted to have a job yesterday. Being friends with time was a chore. I tried to convince myself:

"Eventually, I will be working full time and that will give our family a tight schedule to live by, so, for now Emma and I can benefit from me taking a softer approach."

"There will come a time when I will be a part of the wheel of society."

"I am already contributing since I don't get numbed by the effects of alcohol anymore. I am responsibly partaking in non-profit organisations and have an active roll in the community around us!"

I calmed myself with such thoughts. I tried to listen to

their assessment of me. I focused on the current goals.

Practising being in the here and now, resetting myself as soon as I observed that I was rushing off, daydreaming - which caused myself the pain of yearning.

I wrote, got to be more friends with the internet and using a computer, enjoyed the challenges of my projects at Växa and became more and more comfortable in public places and settings.

Having the chance to take part in the entertainment in our town was also becoming very entertaining, so to speak.

At the age of six, Emma was enrolled at her pre-school, in the autumn of 2007. She was grouped with the children she was to go to school with up until the fifth grade. Those were times to cherish. My pride concerning the development of our little family was something I shared with several other women at Växa and we frequently discussed this area of life with those who worked there. Sometimes, I could notice how I matured from one day to the next. Now and then, I even felt like an adult. But, I was nearing the end of my time at Växa. I was good at keeping my appointments and had completed most tasks I had taken on. Time hadn't allowed for me to pursue a computer certificate which I had been offered to qualify for though, and the driver's license was continuously postponed.

I had practised being flexible when it came to creating time for relaxing in between Emma's school and my time at Växa and our hobbies. Our afternoons were often still occupied with something "to do", this included home-time which I'd realised I had to put as an activity in our schedule. These had also been important goals included in the plan I had made with the professionals involved when I had started at Växa.

It was time to move on in my integration process.

I had an easily-maintainable home and, a laundry room that I could use three times a week, which made things very manageable. To top off all these practical chores, I had a responsible daughter who was a marvel at taking care of things. When I tried to assess my own capacity, I concluded that I ought to be able to work at least four hours, five days per week to begin with. The project leaders agreed with me.

In early 2008 I got to start at Portalen, The Portal, an institution run by the municipality. There, I was assigned an advisor to guide me in getting started in short-term trainee positions in different workplaces. This would not lead to employment but was meant to allow me to try my wings as a worker.

This institution was not only for addicts like myself, but for people who had been without regular work for a long time for different reasons and in need of a slow and closely-guided restart. I signed a contract for two years and we began to sort through viable workplaces. After the two years, my advisor would help me see what I was able to manage, getting an idea of what sector I wanted to work in or whether I was going to choose some sort of education.

Emma became very happy when I told her I was going to start working. Apparently, it was very important to her to have a parent that went to a job like everyone else. This came as a surprise to me. I hadn't known that my six-year-old even thought about things like that. Her reaction was a juicy carrot for me to keep on doing what I had set out to accomplish.

Anna, my advisor, let me contemplate what kind of job I would like to try. She would be visiting me at my job every other week and I would come to her office the other. I felt that it was comforting that I was allowed to take baby steps. I was always welcome to call her and we would both be very aware of how my progress on the road toward regular employment was going.

I told her that I wasn't ready to have to deal with a lot of customers or clients but would probably be best at a job with a physical element to it. She took in what I told her and we discussed possible jobs together. We agreed on an outside job without too many interactions with other people and then she started to look around for me.

The result was that one crisp September morning I got on my bike and pedalled away the four kilometres to a daycare centre for children. There I was going to be the one to take care of the yard, the playgrounds and lawns. Jackpot!

I was always very relaxed around children, the area was very quiet and the grounds were really well-maintained when I started.

I loved it and the months rushed by. Such a practice placement was only meant to last for three months but Emma had fallen ill in the late fall, running high spells of fever on and off for ages. Five months (!) later the doctors figured it out. Strep throat.

Poor child. And poor parent. Phew. I had really gotten the feeling of being a single parent, with the worry, the helplessness and the inability to go to my job. My try-out term was prolonged until the end of March.

When I talked to Anna about this during the period of Emma's illness, she told me about her also having been a single parent to her daughter.

"When she was little I remember the frustration of having to call in sick. I did a lot of VAB-ing in those days."

I didn't know what she was talking about. I had heard this abbreviation before but never understood it. Now I had to ask.

"Oh!" she exclaimed. "Of course it would be unknown to you. It means Vård Av Barn (Care For Child) and is a

benefit one receives from the National Insurance Office."
This was such a normal phrase in our society and most
people had probably learned what it meant already when
they were children.

I actually smiled to myself. Learning something like
this at the age of 42... Sometimes it was quite refreshing
to observe my realisation of how new I was to the world.

Moving on from the outdoor maintenance work was a
natural step to take after that many months. I had become
more comfortable with meeting the people working with
the kids inside the daycare centre. I'd also had a col-
league, a young man, who had worked beside me most
days and this had become a rather nice relationship. Now
and then, several others within the same department
came over to pitch in when we needed more hands and
I had become more relaxed around all these people, even
those I hadn't met before. The time was ripe to move on.

Anna and I sat down again. We talked about what I
could think of doing. It was difficult for me. In the end,
she asked me to tell her of my secret dreams. Without
holding back.

"Hmmm. Writing books." I answered hesitantly, the
corners of my mouth twitching, glancing at her scepti-
cally. I had already decided that writing books was not
an occupation. At least not for me.

"Aaah. Well that's very nice. If I only had that talent,"

she said happily as if that was a real career choice. "Are you good at writing then?" She looked openly at me, smiling matter-of-factly.

I told her of Katja's wonderful feedback and of how the sensation that I ought to be writing had chased me since I was five years old. She nodded and commented, listening, as if writing was something that was normal to be wanting to do.

Now she also brought up the idea of my going to some kind of course to develop my talent. I inwardly shoved that aside, but her words pierced to my core. That she could so uncomplicatedly view writing as an occupation was a bewildering thought. She started up a process inside me where I consciously observed my own way of looking at writing as a "job".

How did a person become an author?

Was it a matter of being discovered or was it a calling?

Did you have to almost go crazy from the yearning to write until there was no other way out?

How big were the risks that an author never followed the talent because of fear or lack of time?

These questions had always been there, in the back of my mind, but when Anna brought this issue to light she had suddenly made them all very clear to me. Deepest down, I really wanted to be an author but I was going to follow the "accepted" path into a working life.

My next workplace was one that would give nourishment to courage and would turn out to help me build a platform for an unwanted and unexpected future I was on the road to meeting.

In early March, Anna and I visited the next place I was going to practise at. Drömmarnas Hus, The House of Dreams, in Malmö. In the borough of Rosengård, the childhood home of our Zlatan Ibrahimovic.

Drömmarnas Hus is an organisation which has its focus on providing workshops and activities for children and young people within the fields of culture, raising questions concerning our society and providing fun and healthy activities.

I would be the spider in the web, working the reception and phone, sorting the mail and making coffee. Just being an available and all-round resource for the house. Cleaning was not my job but rather I had to see to it that the spaces were looking nice and welcoming to visitors, the participants and those working there.

I started in early April 2009 and, from day one, I loved it. My chores were stimulating and the people in the house were inspiring with their dedication and their eagerness to create. I found my place very quickly. I was only working half time but after the long winter with Emma's illness, I was still very exhausted.

This was strange. I often reflected over being so beat. Emma was very "normal" in her need for parenting. Our home was spacious and easy to clean. The laundry room was very easy to gain access to, it was almost as if I had my own washing machine. I ate well and exercised in moderation. I had some minor issues with falling asleep and with waking up at night, but I didn't think that this was anything out of the ordinary. And, still, I didn't seem to have enough time to get everything done.

Anna and I had our regular meetings. I was always very strengthened and I loved to sit and talk to her about work, possibilities and talents. We also talked about routines and things I could improve outside work because these were important factors in allowing for a job to be fitted into my life.

At the end of April, I called Anna and told her I wouldn't be coming to our scheduled appointment at her office that afternoon.

"I can't' make it. I'm completely drained."

The next week we talked at great lengths about what had happened and Anna said she had perceived me as stressed out, as if I was chasing after something or other. She claimed to have seen this for a long time. Even before Drömmarnas Hus. I vaguely remember her mentioning this before but, just as I did with other things sometimes, I had shoved it aside, refusing to hear and now I definitely couldn't understand what she meant.

I fought her words with all my might. The fact that I had called in once to cancel one appointment was not equal to what she described as my "having been unbalanced" for a long while now! I couldn't, wouldn't, relate to this. What she described as the possibility of me being sensitive to stress. Not at all. Not even though others had pointed this out to me too. Not even though I never seemed to have enough time.

I left her office and shook off what we had talked about. I pushed on as usual. If nothing else, I had to prove Anna wrong.

"This doesn't add up." Those words were re-sent over and over in my mind. "It doesn't add up!"

At home, Emma repeatedly pointed out that I was tired and irritable. I wasn't listening. The smallest thing depleted my reserves and I was relieved in April when the warmer weather returned to our southern tip of Sweden. When I was in the sun, I relaxed and the worries of household chores and fitting in all the must do's evaporated.

I was perplexed at how I could be so tired. More often than not, I felt haunted by some undefined worry. Compared to those of many people I knew, my days were very easily organised. I shook these thoughts off and blamed everything and anything between Heaven and Earth for this feeling. The long winter that had seemed much longer because Emma had been ill for so long. The not being used to having a home. The smoking. All the new stuff I was experiencing in life. The list was endless.

But, when it came to the words "sensitive to stress", I bucked wildly.

April eased into May and May into June and my new workplace brought insights into the world of occupations that were amazingly inspiring. To watch these people following their dreams at everything, from project workers to those who lived out their creative ambitions with contributing to non-profit efforts in their free time. The staff in these offices who reached out to sponsors and concert venues, creating events and the two women who were the founders of this organisation supporting the people who participated through all the layers of activities in the house.

Becoming an author was something I couldn't see myself doing but here I got to see people bringing ideas to fruition, ideas which would sound like fantasies at first, but which in time turned into actual events. Well-organised happenings with loads of people involved.

I met all kinds of people. From one who had written plays for children to another who had actually published a book. I met a man who was an artist. I watched the process of him creating an enormous painting together with the children in his group. Theatre plays were being organised from scratch. A team of young men and women between the ages of twenty-five and thirty who coached youngsters into finding their way from an outsider's way of life into daring to dream and start making plans, to finding a workplace. I saw how an information- and PR-campaign came into being before it reached the public.

Seeing what was going on backstage and understanding that it was possible to strive to make real self-invented projects - that was what I was learning here. The chores of my position were things I already knew how to perform and they were done automatically somehow. The real challenge was to take in this truth. People were making their dreams real. Often, these creative individuals had to hold down several jobs at a time to be able to support themselves, everything to create space for their fiery urge to give a thing of beauty to the world. This was what kept them going.

I got to see first-hand that having a cultural occupation truly asked a lot of work from a person. It also became even clearer to me that I would have to wait a long time before I would be able to write my book. First, I had to get as far as having employment.

Every day, I went to work, still on the schedule of four hours a day. Every day, I came home totally worn out. I looked forward to Emma's going to her first summer camp at the end of June where she would be for two weeks. Then I would rest and recuperate and refill my reserves by resting 24/7. Drömmarnas Hus would be closed for the summer and I longed for the light at the end of the tunnel promising fourteen days of revitalising rest.

We began packing Emma's stuff on a Wednesday. The bus for the camp was leaving the following Monday. We both looked forward to this camp in very different ways. Emma was tired of me being tired and she really needed the countryside and getting to play with other kids full-time.

On Thursday morning we were on our way out to go with Emma to her summer pre-school activities and then I was going off to work. When we came outside I discovered that my bike had been stolen.

It would only have been a twenty-minute walk to work, or I could have taken the bus, but I couldn't fathom any of these possibilities. Instead I called in and told the staff member who answered that I would buy a new bike and be in the next day. Somehow I just couldn't break the routine I was used to. I was heavily weighed down by a sensation of demands, as if the whole world depended on me.

I was in luck that day. I found a used bike in a second hand store, incredibly with the original keys to the locks that came with it. I bought it and then I returned home.

Within the walls of our flat, something uncanny began happening to me. I was going into the kitchen when I suddenly lurched into the wall with a loud bang. I observed, as if from afar, that this had occurred quite frequently lately, though not as noticeably. Suddenly I had only tunnel vision. I stood by the counter and the world suddenly became hazy and I got frighteningly numb, affecting all my senses. I was terrified, but wasn't aware that I could call for help. I spent the whole afternoon in an emotional fog. At least I had the presence of mind to call the school to tell them that Emma had to walk home by herself. Whenever I had to move, I fumbled my way around the apartment and when Emma came home I hardly found the words to speak. Fortunately, she was very busy with something she was up to in her room, and she told me later that she didn't notice that I was different that afternoon because she had been used to me being distant and worn out for a long time.

I went to bed early and slept like a log that night. In the morning, nothing was better. Then my fright turned into action. I called Anna and left several messages that she heard when she got into the office at eight. She called me at once.

That conversation is a blurred memory. I stammered, searching for words. Distantly, I heard her telling me to stay at home and to call the hospital. I don't remember if Emma went to the summer pre-school that day.

The hospital told me to stay at home and keep strictly to resting. The weekend passed, I don't remember how but I believe Emma had friends over. On Monday morning, I managed to take her to the bus for summer camp which left just a few blocks from our neighbourhood. Thank God for that summer camp!

I continued being very dizzy and the first week I had big black voids in my brain when I tried to find the words in conversations and at meetings. I did nothing except the bare necessities. Slowly, I got better. Those days are filled with memories patched up from separate events. For all I know, some of these memories might be dreams.

Deep inside, a small sense of recognition started to reverberate, recognition for the nagging of the people around me about my need to slow down. Deep down, on a miniscule scale.

When Emma came back from summer camp I was nowhere near alright but I was on continuous sick leave and had to rest, but only because my body screamed for it. Somehow I managed to patch together our every-day life.

I went to a therapy session at the addiction ward after having had a long break due to the summer vacation. There, my counsellor took my condition very seriously. She claimed that this was a gravely serious health issue. She helped me put what had happened into words and then she concluded that I had possibly crashed from stress.

My mind spun - I couldn't have burnt out. Those two words made me make an ugly face and I spat silently to myself:

"Oh, no you don't!" I shoved it aside with all my might.

She didn't waver though, and referred me to a doctor who specialised in this kind of diagnosis.

I was at the dreaded appointment and was as honest as I could. I didn't want to tell the doctor the truth about how I had felt for the past year, but I did.

"There is no such thing as burning out. That is just a loophole for lazy people! Is there even a clinical diagnosis for it? If there is a scientific medical evaluation for this you had better let me take it!"

I didn't think there would be such a test. Not ever. There was. So instead of me succeeding at sucker-punching a great, big hole in his entire field of expertise, the doctor effortlessly floored me when he matter-of-factly informed me that he would book the appointments to perform such a clinical testing over an eight-month period.

"This reaction to exhaustion is typical of people who, like you, have burnt out. I have heard people call it a lazy people's disease before. Almost without exceptions from people who are workaholics like yourself. You will be assessed over the next eight months, during which you will be on continuous sick leave."

My general condition was very poor, even I had to testify to that, so I just kept my mouth defiantly shut and resigned to just having to show up when he told me to.

The first part of the evaluation process was a series of visits to a counsellor where I got to describe my life and the ways I went about different situations in various areas. How I functioned, so to speak. A saying that I heard when I worked on a ship came to mind:

"I bounce out of bed like a steel spring, set the pace to maximum and get to it, gaining speed as the tough get going!"

It hit me that this mantra had become a slogan of mine through life. I had repeated it out loud often enough through the years. While telling her, I observed my memories of how my job situations had looked in the past. I saw that whether I had been in regular employ-ment or engaged in a criminal endeavour, I had always gone more than all-in. And always while using alcohol as a booster. Narcotics had never worked as a "strength-ener" for me, neither for doing business nor performing tasks at a workplace. I became far too paranoid from them.

When the intoxication wouldn't carry me because of my body rejecting the alcohol, on whichever track I was working at, I changed drugs for a while and then I would find a new job or type of business. And so on and so forth.

For example, when I stole books, I had finally not been able to keep up a good-looking facade and had to recuperate for a while. I had been forced to find other ways to support myself. The same with the smuggling toward the final days when the nervous tension wouldn't be silenced, even by the strongest alcohol types. The same procedure with the legal jobs I'd held down. Maximum pace until I rammed straight into the wall of too much.

I blasted through wall after wall with the igniting solvent of alcohol to hide my true exhaustion. Burning myself to this, a mere crisp of a human being.

A person, having lived a sound and social life, would have a job and co-workers, maybe a family-structure. If that person were in the process of wearing him or herself thin, it would probably be noticed. If not by the person it concerned, most probably the colleagues or family members would point it out and that person would listen. Either begin to slow down of their own accord or going to seek advice from a healthcare professional. Listening to the suggestions given, beginning to take better care of themselves, resting and maybe even taking sick leave. Possibly even a change of career would be necessary.

When I talked to her, looking at my life-long inability to listen to people's remarks concerning my high tempo, I also observed my recurrent refusal to heed my body's signals when I needed to slow down. I sensed a frightening pattern which was unwanted but irrefutably becoming outlined.

The next phase was a series of appointments with a psychologist. There, I performed tests regarding my stamina, concentration- and deduction abilities and if I had any of the letter diagnoses such as ADHD. She also guided me through tests to gather a picture of my general mental state.

During these tests, I noticed that I had changed a lot since my school years. The results and difficulties that arose made me realise that some things didn't function as I expected them to anymore. It was saddening but it also helped me get a truer picture of my abilities. To me, those 25 years had passed very quickly since my life had been very monotonous, with the only gratification being "partying". I was much older, had become slower in my mind, plus I had this difficulty with keeping a manageable pace.

Despite these insights, I got more comfort from these tests than the ones with the counsellor. These were more factual results. They were easier for me to accept than having to change my approach to how I was.

When eight months had passed, the first two parts of the clinical assessment were done. Now there was one short part left. I was to see the doctor who would have reviewed the results together with the counsellor and the psychologist. Based on that material, he and I would sit in sessions where he would interview me to be able to form his professional opinion of my diagnosis.

In the early summer of 2010, the whole examination was finally complete and I sat in my doctor's office to hear the conclusion.

The first thing he told me was that I didn't have any letter combination diagnosis, but I suffered from severe exhaustive depression. He underlined that it wasn't depression as one often thinks of it because I was a very thankful and optimistic person with hope and trust above the average.

"Your basic gratitude is probably because you have survived a deadly disease – your addiction. The kind of depression we are talking about here is solely linked to over-achievement and sensitivity to stress in the context of scheduled work- or other accomplishment-related scenarios." He looked at me to see if I was following. I nodded reluctantly.

"This has nothing to do with your past as an addict. You have exactly the same test results as a female executive we had as a patient here a while back. People had called 112 when they had found her still standing outside her car exactly where she had stood four hours earlier. She stood there with her hand on the door, in the rain, for four hours, unable to move," he peered at me again, my lower lip started to twitch. The cramp in my throat was unbearable.

"You are an intelligent person and that is something that can be an imposition for you with this type of personality. You have no brake-system whatsoever and have driven yourself into far too many brick walls in your lifetime. With having used alcohol as a boosting fuel over the years, you have crossed far too many borders where others would have crashed a long time ago. I cannot see how you would be able to recuperate from this. Not in any foreseeable future. You cannot burden an employer with this hyper-sensitivity to stress. You will have to seek early retirement and we will back you up 100 percent."

I cried. I knew. I hadn't improved since the crash last year, but to get this lain out for me in such plain wording made it written in stone somehow.

"This would have come your way whether you had been an alcoholic or not," he nodded as if to himself looking through my papers. He looked up, a bit bewildered when he saw me smiling at him through the veil of tears.

"It was good to hear it out loud, even though it is awful, completely awful." I hiccupped.

There was a warm, consoling feeling stirring in my gut – at least I hadn't drugged all my chances down the drain as I had feared.

One of the worst symptoms of the disease of addiction is the delusion of being an outsider. I had lived almost all my life with that lie between my ears. It had been there before I used alcohol for the first time. It was the reason that alcohol had become my best friend - I wasn't capable of relating to people. Now, I had met so many other recovering addicts and seen them recovering and when the first healing of the body and mind had stabilised, most of these acquaintances got into education or workplaces quite soon. But me, I had still borne the stigma of the outsider, even in these circles. Now I got to know that I had an archetype of the personality of those who burnt out. I was "normal" within the group of people who crashed like me.

Paradoxically, this was a comforting thought!

Nevertheless, this is a bottomless sorrow for me. Afterwards, I have met many others who view this diagnosis as a loop-hole for the lazy – all of them are like me. At the same time, there are people who know there is such a thing as burn-out and from time to time they still have to flag me down. I forget that this is what I suffer from and start pushing on again. But now these frenzied active booms can last a couple of hours maximum. If I don't slow down in time I become completely drained. So I try to remember to take it easy, every single day.

I have to have a nap at least once a day to have the brain reset the level of stress hormones. I can't just sit on the sofa and relax. My brain is on constant alert. The exhaustion drags me down several times daily and this is the evidence I comfort myself with as proof that I'm not lazy. But then I forget again and try to achieve more than I am able to.

I still have hopes and dreams and we will see. Time will tell.

In the autumn of 2009, four months after my crash and noticing that I hadn't gotten any better, the evaluation from Anna at Portalen dropped into the letterbox. I wasn't going to be let back. She had spoken to my doctor. In the midst of this inconsolable sorrow, there shone a light in my innermost reaches. I turned to my keyboard. I began to write. I had to have something to do, you see.

For Emma, this has been a difficult situation. If she needed the support of others before because of her traumatic childhood, she certainly needed it now. It has been very important for her to have routines, but with a parent with an exhaustive disorder, this has not always been possible.

She has seen me writing and when one book after the other became successful and I began participating in public talks and discussions, often with media coverage, she began to understand that I was doing something, if ever so moderately, that was important. It was essential for her to see that I was a productive parent, even if my occupation didn't have the normality of a 9 to 5.

Also, she has developed an understanding for my disability. With time.

Emma has also been affected by my refusal to accept this as my reality. I think she realised the truth long before I did. As children often do...

She also helped me see that being an author, even if I am not able to take part in everything I want to, is an important job and that books are essential to many people, including us, who love to read for both recreational and learning purposes.

Emma also has a true knack for writing herself. Maybe it is the observant writer inside her that sees what I often am blind to.

I let three years pass before I sent my early retirement application to be filed with the National Insurance department. I thought I knew better than my doctors. I thought I would get better.

I do get better. At accepting that this is for life.

I do get better. At resting and at keeping a very sparsely-booked calendar.

I have learned to plan, rest before and after I have scheduled events which I participate in. I need to be rigorously disciplined to be able to do things outside the home. And I have to. I would shrivel up if I didn't get to participate in the world around me.

I do talks and discussions, I blog rarely but heartily - and I write.

I practise every day at leading a full life despite being locked down by daily spells of fatigue and periodical insomnia. I have an occupation even if it's not what I'd imagined it would look like.

We both took a huge step forward in coming to terms with this in 2015 when I was finally able to back down. The acceptance suddenly took off, helping me descend several notches at once.

I am learning to lead a life of being a resource without having a fixed routine. This is finally beginning to sink in.

Then life happens and there are things I have to do or situations that occur over which I am powerless and then I see, very clearly, what my doctor meant about me not being able to have employment.

In the dark of night when sleep eludes me.

When the big black reaches, the aftershocks of exhaustion swim,

Where dreamlands ought to have had free, unfenced ranges.

That's when I write.

I reflect. I tell tales. I ask a lot of questions.

I write for the love of my humanity, I write for the love of all things human.

I have written my books. I have a dream that I'm not allowed to say out loud, I'm not even allowed to think it, but I can write it down for you, Dear Reader:

I hope to contribute, with my story and thoughts, to the ongoing worldwide spreading of hope. To pitch in and tell people of the truth that millions upon millions of people are recovering from the disease of addiction. The hope that young people showing the symptoms of social withdrawal early, thanks to having information on recovery being possible, seek help without having had to be savaged by drugs as a substitute for human companionship. Without having had to lead harmful and shredded existences as I did.

Dare I say this? Yes! I dream of being a part of making this world a better place. And I am. Only by being sober am I giving back instead of only taking. I am pitching in.

There! I just proved my doctor's point. No brake-system. Whatsoever...

I have a desire to always be in the process of occupational development through channels available to me and thus contributing to the co-existence of us, this, our wondrous humanity.

Relationships

My viewpoint was always that of an outsider looking in. It was impossible for me to take the steps that would let me experience inclusion. When I was little, I wasn't aware of being different - that was just the way I had always been. I was there, amongst family and friends, but unable to join in.

Now I know that all children need to take awkward steps into being active members of the surrounding world, and for most this development comes from guidance from adults and from interacting with friends. But I never took those steps and didn't find a comfortable place in that sphere of togetherness, cosiness and fun. It was a zone where everyone else seemed so at home, so naturally enjoying and benefitting from each other's company.

In those earliest years, neither my family nor I realised that I was socially stumped. Of late, people have told me that they hadn't noticed my extremely strong feeling of being an outsider. But I seldom showed or expressed my actual emotions. I kept up communication on the track I'd learned by mimicking the expected reactions and responses. Seemingly calm and present, but often when I was in the company of others I was ridden by overwhelming, rugged emotions inside. Painful surges in their intensity. The biggest problem was that I was incapable of finding any kind of healthy outlet for these emotional storms.

The effect of the drugs only gave a desperate substitute for a state of belonging.

Without belonging, I might as well not exist. The deadly, suicidal obsession of the illusory completeness which is the effect of drugs. All the hellish consequences I caused instead of "simply" having learned to interact with other people.

Actually, I came to an understanding of my social disorder as late as in my fortieth year when I began to understand what I was actually recovering from. During my whole life, no one around me had known either. Now my family and I do know that recovery is possible. Now I am learning to take my wobbly steps in all my relationships. It is quite scary but I pray for courage and I do it. One precious day at a time.

Looking back at my looking on at the others enjoying companionship, where everything seemed so simple and relaxed, I can see that my blockage was almost total. I couldn't tune into their connecting vibes. I could take part for a while, but as soon as the uncomfortable tension became too tough to bear inside, if I had the opportunity to leave, I would take it. And that always happened sooner or later.

My longing to belong was there, throbbing deep down,

but it was subconscious. As no child consciously does, I never knew that belonging in a social context was a cornerstone of being human. When the yearning to be a part of humanity twirled restlessly inside me, I didn't automatically search out another person to be with. I didn't see companionship as being the missing ingredient. I had no natural pull to interact beyond satisfying my basic needs of food, drink and sleep.

I baked myself into a safe cocoon and communicated with the world around me through acting, with controlled, ostensibly functioning responses.

I would have been relieved if I had shared what was going on inside me with another human being. But my dysfunction made me scared and I instinctively shut other people out. Eventually, the pain that comes with isolation became so great that I grasped desperately onto any other outlet than the one that truly would have worked.

Desperate quick fixes always won over communicating with another person. I didn't know how to. This was the core ability I didn't know how to use.

In social contexts, I got very worn out from being just an observer when I was thought to be a participant. It took lots of energy to respond acceptably and correctly without actually being able to relate to people. So instead of learning to communicate, I learned to read people.

I was socially impaired and when a small child learns a new language to communicate with, it learns it flawlessly. This was also the case for me in learning this art and, since I was on my own, I learnt communication in my own way.

I played the part, talking and smiling in the manner I had observed others doing and I was very convincing. This was how I developed the uncanny trait of manipulation – and with a child's perfect ability to copy. I learned to play the part of human interaction in an impeccable manner, performing in a believable way, which not even the finest acting schools in the world can teach their pupils. It was my way of communicating.

I'd always thought that this was how everyone was. Disconnected from one another. I didn't know anything else.

Despite all this, I was always thought to be a very socially competent person. All through my life there were very few times when I didn't create a talkative and pleasant atmosphere. I was just never really there...

The idea that I was different began to stir in my conscious mind as I got a little older. I remember having the first clear thoughts about this when I was around 10, give or take a year or two. I began consciously backing away from the unknown territory of interacting with the people around me, but this had the opposite effect to the relaxation I was after. In hindsight, I see that isolation only worsened my emotional strain. And, of course, being a child, I didn't know where this agony had its roots. The subconscious starvation from missing relationships grew, which in turn furthered my separation from others. The unknown terrain of co-existing and the strangeness of the world began to scare me and I countered the fear by building defences. Thick, armoured walls consisting of theories as to why I didn't need anyone in my life.

I was most at ease when adventure soared through me. A captivating book, maybe an outing on challenging terrain or some other physical activity that demanded my whole focus. Anything that upped my endorphins. Most preferably, I wanted to be alone on these flights.

The sport that caught me was swimming and my favourite hobbies were books and snorkelling. The lone wolf going strong.

As a five-year-old, I found the thing with the greatest potential for making me feel at home in this strange world. I tasted alcohol and wanted to do it again.

I have met quite a few people who had their first contact with alcohol at a very early age but didn't have the same experience of its effects as I did. My life's future rut was lain out within seconds. The foundation of a path was drawn, heading straight toward a destiny that I could never have pictured myself living when I grew up.

I remember clearly those first times with alcohol in my system. The extreme sensation of belonging. Freed, not having to be alert, liberated from the constant reading of my surroundings. Within seconds I suddenly felt powerfully relaxed around others.

The relief from my emotional strain was astounding. Being able to sit back, my constant subconscious interpreting of people's facial expressions and analysing their tones of voice was turned down. The freedom was exhilarating.

Of course, I didn't realise at the time what this minty-fresh breath of emotional relaxation was about. But now I can see this effect clearly being a major factor throughout my life in relation to alcohol. This drug was able to induce a chemical substitute, causing me to experience feelings I couldn't have with people. Feelings of fitting in, at last.

But this sensation was chemically triggered. Never lasting very long because my body fought with all its might to break down the poison and this "bliss" always came with a price. What I experienced wasn't even real because it wasn't the result of a developed ability.

I now know that the effect I was depending on alcohol giving me was that of belonging, because I recognise it when I get that wondrous feeling today. That remarkable touch of being at home, which occurs when I truly interact with another person.

Without the filter of a buzz, when the harmony is pure and no longer drug-related, it stays with me and doesn't take a toll on me. It just gives my life wealth beyond my wildest dreams. Thriving and growing companionship.

So, I never knew, and no one suspected, that anything was amiss. As I am told, I was very sociable. But the tell-tale signs ought to have been clear when alcohol became a prominent companion in my life. If knowledge of the symptoms of the disease of addiction had been widespread, my obsession with alcohol would have revealed my social dysfunction. I find solace in believing that this characteristic of this terrible affliction will be acknowledged in the future. I even hope that an education in social development will be introduced in schools. Turning the tides on repeated generations of social dysfunction.

When I turned 14, I left home for boarding school. Because of the strong impulse which drew me to the quick-fix of the chemically-induced haven, the natural yearning for co-existing with people was continuously subdued. Instead, the agony of my disorder intensified the hunt for the deafening effects of alcohol. I lost the ability to reach any pure feeling of belonging other than when my innermost being managed to break through, wanting something else, but this only lasted for very short bursts. Mostly, these bursts could be counted in seconds.

Without any insight into the true nature of my inability to relate, I relished the soothing and enhancing buzz of alcohol. Ruthlessly driven by an impulse that overrode the memories of the bad consequences I had caused. Unmoved by all the people I was shrugging off after having trampled over them. No sane person could be as single-minded as I was. It was as if I suffered from dementia – blind to every consequence.

I followed the superficial and dangerous lie of drug-induced contentment. The buzz of having found my place on Earth.

Something I always refuted as a cliché was sadly my truth – the bottle was my best friend. I followed it through thick and thin, and as long as I had it with me I needed no other. In fact, I was incapable of relating to people at all as long as I had alcohol in my life.

But a human being belongs with other human beings, and not with a chemical substance. That was still, of course, the only truth. And deep, deep down inside, my yearning for true companionship lay there, smouldering, disturbing the lie I was living.

One of my most painful memories comes from a period

during the later years of my active addiction. This sprang from a dream which had begun to recur. The hungover misery had started waking me very early in the mornings, but suddenly, instead of the hunt beginning to fire up inside me, I was filled with a warm, cosy feeling. Pulsating emotional waves of inclusion, an experience of fellowship and intimate friendship ties. The sensation was very intense. I had shared laughter, fun and sorrow with people in my sleep and awoke with memories of affection that gladdened me in the core of my being. This was something I hadn't been able to experience in real life for ages. I had a few vague recollections of this kind of togetherness from my early years with my family, and a very few with friends before things got totally helter-skelter, but other than that, nothing.

Before I woke up and became fully aware of the real world, the emotions I bathed in were the sweetest I'd had in decades. The most painful and agonizing thing about them was that they were about "Friends". Literally it was me and the characters from the TV show.

When it sank in how my day had really started, it stabbed me in the gut. It was like a rugged knife twisting in my soul.

I wasn't stupid. In those dazed minutes before being wide awake, I agonisingly saw that these dreams were rooted in a deep-set longing for taking part, for communing with others. Then I swallowed my first sips and soon I was guffawing, making a great effort to laugh it all off, ridiculing these dreams, or rather, the feelings these dreams brought up to the surface. But it didn't work.

The want for belonging wasn't that easily quenched. This sprung from an immensely powerful human building block that I was lacking. My agony came from grave emotional famine.

These nightly oases of playfulness and joy came to me in the middle of a terribly downward spiral. This was during the period when I was admitted to hospital for alcohol detox on several occasions. I had begun doubting myself and my invincibility. My "best friend" was abandoning me and my existence, the relationship-starved existence I was leading stared me straight in the face. I refused to acknowledge it when I was awake but kept rigorous focus on the mirage of the buzz.

This was just before I became pregnant.

When Emma came into the world, my social disorder, at the core of my disease of addiction, became much more difficult to turn away from. She was clear in her signals, reaching out to me with her emotional sonar, but her pings only bounced back unanswered from my mute and disabled receiving and responding end. My inability became a disturbingly persistent gnawing inside and her needs to communicate went unanswered due to my underdeveloped emotional capacities.

My inner strength was deafened and I began spending maybe a couple of minutes instead of seconds doubting the "choice" of my habits. On top of this, the effects of my soul-mate, alcohol couldn't take the edge off Emma's need for me. I couldn't bear to look at this. I kept on using and fought to get through every day. The filter between reality and myself stood out more clearly every day. My idea of alcohol being strengthening and fun was now constantly being challenged by its true nature which was that it made me even more unattainable. The intoxication had only delivered me farther away from social ability ever since the first time I tried it.

The more I fought to defend my way of life, the harder and thicker my armour became.

During my daughter's first four years, emotions began developing within me as never before. Very, very slowly, but undeniably very surely. I felt the inadequacy I showed toward my child. Even my own family began stating the obvious – that I wasn't acting as a healthy person would. I refused to admit what they pointed out. But their words lingered. Their obvious love and care for us stung me.

Finally, in the last months of my active addiction, these emotions crystallized into thoughts and I was able to express the fact that I didn't have the social tools to relate, not even to my most beloved person. I let the municipality take care of my daughter. I resigned to being incapable of having a sound relationship with another person, not even my wondrous little girl.

There, the pain of moving toward exchanging alcohol for living in the real world began. The worst life-sucking substance was tragically what I had used as a crutch instead of being with others. I had let this disabling drug be what hosted me in my socially tentative blundering. I hadn't known better and not many around me had had the understanding of how tragic this drug was. I stopped using this antisocial filter and became sober.

I now embarked on a journey to get to know the most ignored person in my life. It took all the courage I could muster. I had to get in really close. To know this person was to know others. I asked for help and then I started to nudge this loveable one.

I started to get to know myself.

It's not important whether or not I was different from the start or even if I was ever. The only important thing is that I believed that I was.

Reality around me was distorted by the effects of the drug. My perceptions in that mind-altered state fortified the picture of myself as unusual. Towards the end, these misinterpretations were almost irrefutable in my chains of thought. But only almost. Somewhere deep inside, an inborn bell tolled with a resonance which echoed in tune with the rest of humanity. When I began to recover, this tone, the one of fellowship, urged me on and bred the urge to taste more of life. Life in the purest form I had ever known.

The first time this stood out was only a few days after I had stopped using alcohol and I was at the market in my borough buying fruit. A market seller behind the green, red and yellow mounds of healthiness smiled at me, making a joke. The glint in his eyes and the vibe of his friendly communication speared straight through my wall. I was absolutely taken aback and almost literally took a step backwards. In a split second, I was completely amazed that I hadn't been reachable before. I instantly realised that this was what it was to be part of humanity.

39 years old and I woke up with a small child's self-centred outlook and the journey to learn how to maintain healthy relationships seemed like a life-long project. Thankfully, I was lured by the idea of a life filled with exchanges, challenges and everything else that was new. These were ingredients in life which I had missed out on through always leaning on alcohol to carry me. Now I was to learn and grow as a person instead of being physically depleted and mentally stagnated.

This attracted me more than words can say.

The first summer, Emma was still living with a foster family and I filled these months with teenage stuff. I learned to converse without being tipsy, I listened to music loudly and wore my headphones everywhere. I rode my bike all hours and went to festivals and music events, amazed at feeling great at 2 a.m.

Daily, I met lots of people, talked to them and even if this was mostly around the self-help organisations and not so much privately, it was still meeting people. Wondrous reality!

Like the relative from the countryside who feels lost in the big city, I took my first careful steps into the world of grown-ups, without a clue as to what to expect. Thankfully, the conversations I had with the people in the twelve-step fellowship were deeper that the ones I had with people in other settings. This meant that I got practice at socialising on an intimate level very early on, despite the fact that I had just gotten to know the people I was talking to.

Sometimes, voices inside me began chattering about what I had said or what I ought to have said and what not to say again. Did, ought to and ought not. This inner critic often began by putting me down concerning my inabilities at socializing.

The gratitude toward the mind-blowing changes I had made and all the things I was achieving kept this voice down though, and every time, it lost the battle of luring me back into isolation.

I kept on challenging myself to join in with humanity.

The love I showed myself in taking on these challenges was a huge step in my getting to know me, the most important person in my life.

I realised that getting to know myself would give me the tools I needed to be a good parent. The logic in attaining a good sense of self would be what would carry me as a mother, as a fellow human being and in a possible future, as a lover in a relationship with a partner. I spoke silently to myself in strong, encouraging sentences when I hurled myself into these nauseatingly scary and daring social endeavours.

I realised that I would have to maintain my social ability throughout my life and early on I put this down as the most important 'note to self'. I noticed that numerous people shared about having similar experiences in the self-help group.

The near-instinctive pull towards isolation was such an early-learnt pattern in me that it would probably always be my first impulse. But the joy of finally having relationships with others made me befriend this experience as a priority in my new life.

I believed that these people talked from their own experience. The sharing that came from those who had lived sober for a long time and who I had noticed were actually living good lives now, made me rely on what I heard.

If recovery had been thought up by just a couple of people or by some professional "expert" sitting in a room creating sentences that looked good on paper, chaining together logical deductions about my disorder, I wouldn't have been helped. Listening, seeing and finding what rang true within me from others who had found and who lived in a solution was what worked. I was so thankful for having found a well-practised way out of the crazed hell-hole I had lived in. I was finding solid ground on Earth. At last.

To see these recovering addicts living a life freed from alcohol and other drugs, listening to them telling similar tales, sharing the joy of building loving lives and recovering year after year – this was what gave me hope and practical knowledge I could weigh up to see if it suited me and Emma.

I wasn't different. There wasn't anything especially unusual about me. This was a haven of loving acceptance and true evidence of recovery. There I sank my anchor. This was where I learned to relate to being a human among humans.

I now had a soaring image of myself as a unique individual, as everyone is, but where the apartness was erased. This gave me courage. For a person who was so malnourished in the human sphere the moments when I felt fellowship with others were by far the most valuable I had ever experienced.

The bottle's false comfort would never again be able to compete with the sensation I got when I was naturally relaxed around people. At least not as long as I kept nourishing this newfound ability and was disciplined in my plan to meet people.

I caught myself daydreaming about the things I hoped to do in the future and was surprised when these plans always included family and friends. I was determined to never again become the stagnated, self-centred and shut-off person I had been. I wanted, with all my heart, to be a part of society. When I viewed the world around, I belonged, and the co-hell-ision I had seen before was no longer my truth.

Luckily, I was in the middle of the forest and didn't realise how many trees there were. I still don't. The path through the woods is a winding one but is lightly tread when fuelled by the joy of finally being in true contact with the people in it. Companionship gives me the contentment that the effect of alcohol was only a poor substitute for.

I went about practising the art of mingling as best as I could before the time when Emma was going to move back with me. As a single mother of a five-year-old I wouldn't get the same opportunities to try my wings. So, at the same time as missing her immensely and putting much time into seeing her, I devoted every other second to learning to hang around with other people. Even to call these attempts baby-steps would probably be rated an overstatement to an on-looker, but to me these ventures into the big, wide world were like a giant's leaps.

I went to the addictive ward at the hospital seven days a week, visited Emma at the orphanage and later at the family home with Mona and Ulf, her foster parents. I went to the self-help meetings, for coffee with friends and I had Växa to go to too.

Swedish people are the most sociable in Europe according to surveys. Not because we talk to each other in public places, which we scarcely do with people we don't know, but Sweden has an infinite number of non-profit organisations and almost everybody is a member of one or more of them and, there, we meet lots of people.

These democratic groupings range from outdoor recreational activity-lovers to carpet-weaving enthusiasts. Aquarium nerds, blind people's activity fellowships, rave or folk-music fans. People who have moved to Sweden from abroad often create organisations where they can meet. In every likely and unlikely field, you can find some non-profit grouping or other. On top of the activities the members can partake in, these associations are also a schooling in democracy at a hands-on level.

One of the largest and of great importance in Sweden is Hyresgästföreningen – The Swedish Union of Tenants. With 530 000 households as members, several million Swedish people reap the benefits of membership of this non-profit organisation. The vision is to secure housing that promotes human and social development - so that all people can have the right to good housing at affordable costs. In this day and age, when humanity is still letting profit count for more than our very lives, this is an organisation that truly keeps a real esteem of every person's basic rights in the foreground. Among the benefits are tenant-related legal aid and support but also stores and the opportunity to take part in a lot of activities at a discount. Such benefits range from cinema tickets and participation in different other non-profits to pet-shop products and floral gifts.

I was, among a few others, a member of a nation-wide fitness movement called Friskis and Svettis - Healthy and Sweaty, and a couple of national sobriety organisations (not counting the twelve-step fellowships - they follow other, global, traditions) and, of course, Hyresgästföreningen.

The months passed quickly. I had gotten a lot further on in knowing myself in relation to others when Emma was suddenly home. For the first time in our lives together, the light of my life and I were living in a sane universe.

We talked all the time. We went for outings, too many in the beginning as it turned out. At home we did a lot of things together.

I noticed that we were very alike in our social development skills. She was five and I was 40. I could see myself in her when she carefully estimated the steps she took in interacting with others, daring to venture outside the little child's self-centred sphere. Revolving in her own tiny universe was no longer enough. I could relate to her explorations among the people in the surrounding world, prying into the mannerisms of another person. I was also tentatively exploring outside the worn-down fortress I had always kept myself within.

After a couple of years she had surpassed me. It was clear that Emma had a natural capability for co-existing. Without seeming to feel peculiar, she grew in her interactions with others. I was still uncomfortable at times and had to keep a disciplined approach to the art of being social, easily drawn to isolation as I was. If I went out or invited people home, I enjoyed it but it didn't come naturally. I prayed for the courage to bring this up with someone and then I talked about my difficulties with a friend. She nodded and then agreed with a heartfelt:

"Mmm. Exactly."

I didn't say anything but waited for her to elaborate on that. In my mind, I had pictured that this talk would develop into her telling me exactly how I should act to become the perfectly synchronised mother, friend and future partner. Possibly also give me clues of how to become an ultimate "girl-talk"-wizard, a talent which I imagined that every "normal" woman ought to master. And, last but not least, she would reveal to me how I was to become the centre of attention at the upcoming trend-setting social gatherings everyone attended, just like the ones you see in the movies.

Instead, her tone of voice had sounded just as average as I felt. "Mmm. Exactly". After eyeing me quizzically, realising I wanted more from her, she continued:

"This isn't an easy chapter. I go through the same thing. All the time. How many times I've fantasized about how much happier I would be if I had lots of female friends. Something always held me back though, and with time I've developed a few close friendships. I've realised that huge circles aren't for me. I've found joy and comfort with being a low-key person. I guess that's the same as most people in the world. Some do want to have a large group of friends, but that's not me. The friends I have I love dearly but I don't hang out with them all that much. I spend a lot of time with my family, my interests are in a couple of organisations and my work and I've travelled a few times. This has turned out to be the life I find exciting and I love it. Boring, huh?" Then she winked at me and laughed.

The happiness that shone through her words made me

re-evaluate my fixed ideas of what a grown-up woman's life should be like, including the regular, dressed-up mingling, and all that. Being a regular down-to-Earth mother, café-going friend and wearing comfy clothes suddenly seemed a quite wonderful womanhood to aspire to.

I gave a lot of thought to what made others happy in their relationships. Emma seemed to be very happy with getting my undivided attention for about one or even half an hour every day. Other than that, she easily filled her life with friends, projects and adventure.

I studied one of my sisters who often arranged couch-get-togethers as one of her most valued quality-time activities with her friends.

My sponsor suggested that I take hour-long walks by myself in the soothing environments which Malmö teems with. I began strolling in the parks and along the several kilometres of beaches we have. She often reminded me to nourish my relationship with myself and to be aware of showing myself love and care.

Sometimes when I saw the beauty and ease other people seemed to have in their relationships, it brought me to thinking that I would never be capable of feeling comfortable in the various settings I imagined other people thrived in. Once again, the self-help meetings were a priceless resource to me. I kept on getting back on track, to a sense of belonging and normalcy, as long as I listened and trusted what I heard there. I topped up my hope account and settled my feet back in the midst of humanity. Resetting my real place.

*

I allowed myself to grieve my disorder.

I seemed to have a barrier that went up, mostly without warning. I could find myself instinctively surfing on a mental and emotional plateau, shifting in evasive manoeuvres, preventing me from touching any ground with the company I was subjected to at that moment.

The only thing to do when I discovered myself doing this was to reinstate my presence. Recapturing the here and now.

When I was into my third year of recovery, I began to befriend this tendency for alienation. I had to. It seemed close to instinctive for me to react in that way and I didn't get better at it, whether I hated this behaviour or not, so I decided that accepting it was the most loving thing I could do for myself. Once again, self-centredness stood out as a massive core ingredient in my affliction. Everyone experiences troubles and insecurities in relating, but this abnormally strong self-centredness caused an intense emotional reaction which I felt as actual physical pain. With that there came an extreme experience of truly being alien from other people.

This vulnerability was a state I had never allowed myself to acknowledge earlier in life. The illusory protection that alcohol had offered had proven itself to be a lie. Now I stood without the thing which I had always put my life in the hands of. Instead, I turned to the inner resources of trust, gratitude and hope which I found more powerful than the drug. The attraction of these loving traits lifted me and allowed me to experience safety and strength in a way that beer had never allowed me to.

If I remembered to summon these strong, loving principles, I knew I would always feel included, whatever my disease tried to deceive me into "thinking".

In waves throughout life, I will probably get into something similar to the development phases of a teenager. This was necessary for me to accept early on in my recovery.

Always being in the process of learning how to have conversations, always being brave at getting to know new people, being sincerely jovial, not talking about dancing or worse, flirting - and all this without the crutch of alcohol. Trembling, sweaty, unfathomably vulnerable moments, when the heart is beating dangerously close to jumping out of the chest and invisibility stealth-suits seem to be the most crucial invention for mankind.

Situations when the embarrassment of running away

is the only thing pinning my feet to the ground making me stay. Eternal moments when a strange look spreads across my reddening face and choking thoughts of the worldwide doom I would face for being a champion fool that chased me for ages afterwards.

These emotional rollercoasters still befall me in the strangest situations. It can happen without reason in the elevator, maybe when I am with people I don't know very well or when talking to a cashier at the store. Doing a public talk is nowhere near as squirmingly agonizing as when this happens in close encounters.

I have gotten better with time but suddenly I'm there again. I find comfort in knowing that many people feel like this and I have gotten some practice at keeping a neutral expression despite what's going on inside.

My father helped me to look at this when he said that almost everyone thinks that others have better self-esteem than they do. When I find myself wanting to disappear, I often use this as an affirmation to return to the here and now.

I smile at thinking about what people around me can't see me boosting myself with sometimes in social situations.

*

I waited for the longest while before I even considered

dating. Well, at least after those first two obsessions in my early recovery when, thankfully, I was turned down. I had hardly known who I was back then. But then he entered the scene. At first I just became annoyingly distracted sometimes without understanding why. Then I began noticing that this only happened to me when he was around. Curiosity won over wanting to disappear from the face of the Earth when I saw him, and the wheels began to turn.

I had known him for several years but we hadn't spoken much. Now it was the late summer of 2011 and I had been in recovery for five and a half years. Many of the pieces of a good routine and everyday life had fallen into place and my relationships with myself, Emma and the surrounding world had been stabilising noticeably the last year or so. Then suddenly, he stormed in – The One in Shining Armour. We had never met in tête-a-tête before. During that spring and summer we ran into each other in places we had never seen each other in before. Several times. It was truly quite strange. This happened often. Emma and he actually got to spend enough time together to get to know each other during these completely random "just-happening-to-be-in-the-same-place-at-the-same-time"-encounters.

Something stirred inside at one of these occasions and an uneasy insight rose to the surface.

"I have never flirted sober!" This thought came before

I had consciously suspected that the tingle I felt was something more than just friendly comradeship. Now I understood and life became the unruly Wild, Wild West in a second.

I summoned courage and then asked him to come over to talk about a project which we were cooperating on in a non-profit organisation. When he said he would rather meet up at a café or at the place where we were doing the project, I dared put my foot down. Evenings were the time of day which suited us and I stressed Emma's need for me at home, which wasn't entirely true – but desperate times called for desperate measures! We decided that he would come over a few days later.

He came, we talked about the project for five minutes and then we discussed life, the universe and everything for more than an hour until he suddenly realised that he had to leave. The hour had flown past and I realised that it was way past Emma's bedtime. I could see that he had enjoyed himself too.

When we stood in the hallway and he was tying his shoes I thought to myself:

"Okay. If he doesn't ask me out now I'll call him this week, ask him to have a coffee with me and tell him that I'm asking him out on an actual date!"

Then he began fidgeting, looking at his shoes and shifting his weight from one foot to the other.

"Errr. Have you ever seen The Smurfs in 3D?" He

glanced at me.

I smiled widely. How cute was that? Emma was in the equation and he looked so sweet! (Read - handsome and brave!)

"Weeell, er, no. Not really. Have you?!"

"I go to the movies a lot."

"Okay. It sounds like fun. Why don't we go?"

I had a dizzy spell and had to hold on to a chair. I don't think he saw it. I got my bearings and quickly asked, in case he changed his mind:

"I know that Emma would love to see it. Is that what you were thinking, that we would all three of us go?"

They had already eaten hotdogs and ice creams together that summer and had had lots to talk about.

"Of course," he smiled. "So we'll do it then?"

"Absolutely!" I smiled with my whole face.

We decided to talk over the phone to arrange the time and place. I embraced him a little longer than for a usual friendly hug and then he left. The era of waiting set in.

He called the next day and we decided on a week from then. Luckily, my father and his new sweetheart were arriving the next day. They were coming down from Dalarna to stay with us for five days. This was a social occasion which meant very much to Emma and me. The days crawled by from wanting to see him again but for once, waiting was a good thing. Otherwise, with such a wonderful family reunion, those days would probably have flown by - it was the first time my father had been to our home. Also he and his sweetheart were very much in love and to watch them flirting and giggling fuelled my hope for romantic love, even for me who had passed 40.

I made up my mind to enjoy the mere state of infatuation and then the wait became painfully sweet, even when the minutes seemed to pound at my soul. I distracted myself with writing: I was in the last stages of fine-tuning the original Swedish version of "I Only Wanted to Dance", "Jag ville bara dansa". I also took the time to enjoy the crispy autumn days with my visiting family.

At long last, The Day came and we met up at the cinema to pick up the tickets and then, before seeing the picture, we went for dinner together.

We had been acquainted for a long time and had many interests in common so we had lots to talk about, but the tension at this stage was very noticeable. We were both nervous which felt comforting to me. The days that had passed since I'd seen him last had been packed with questions such as whether he "liked me", or not. If he actually just felt like going to the movies, or not. If I would dare to get into a couples relationship, or not.

Emma went to refill her dessert and then he said something about losing his ability to speak now that he wanted to impress me. I said something about him being very sweet. A small light flickered in the storm I sensed between us when we had said these few words, smiling into each other's eyes. Deliberating silently, I decided to ask him, straight out, when we walked to the cinema. After Emma had finished her dessert, we left.

I hooked my arm into his, summoned courage by saying a split-second prayer and then I just did it:

"Do you want to see me again? I mean, like, on a date? Because I would really like that. I feel a very strong attraction to you – you are a very likeable man."

He smiled and looked at me:

"Of course I would. Absolutely. I'm very attracted to you too."

I squeezed his arm.

"Yes!" I said and grinned happily back at him.

Emma, who had been skipping along ahead of us, suddenly bounced back, as if her radar had clearly picked up on an anomaly, something like something realigning in the solar-system.

"What??! What did you say? What's going on?"

He ruffled her hair.

"Want some candy for the movie?"

She twitched her grin and through thin slits she studied us silently with a look on her little face that said: "Ok, I'll let you have your secret... For now".

"Yupp. Give me lots of candy, please." Then she bounced off again, twirling and running backwards, shouting: "Are you going steady now then, or what?"

We laughed out loud and answered in unison:

"Yes, we are." And then I raced her all the way to the theatre.

I became insanely infatuated. When Emma and I went to Tenerife a month later, it was unbelievably agonizing to leave him behind. It wasn't only the missing my Prince Charming that ached in my body and soul during the three weeks we were away. I had also decided earlier that year to end the relationship with the last of my "best friends" from the life-threatening drugs group. I was quitting nicotine. I had quit smoking the year before but now it was time to be free for real. That "holiday" was a struggle that I will never put myself through again. Which means I will never pick up nicotine in any form. Ever! The lie of the Marlboro man will not fool me again!

The surges of infatuation triggered endorphins. Fighting the nicotine addiction kicked up the adrenalin. Well, probably both hormones went haywire from both of these mad processes twirling in competition with each other inside. My insides were screaming out to be listened to constantly. This was a recipe for a most busy vacation. I actually got to relax when we got home again.

My fiancé and I still don't live together even if we often stay over at each other's places. We both take care to keep up our individual hobbies and interests. I didn't waver about continuously putting my recovery first.

But, of course, as the doctors claim we all do, I became insane with infatuation. Poisoned by the bodily hormones of love. Since having managed the first two years of recovery with everything concerning Emma's moving and coming home, this was the most turbulent emotional craze I'd had.

It was a big change for Emma too. From having had me all to herself, she suddenly had to share me and even when she and I were alone I was often distracted. It was as I could imagine having had a teenage crush would be like, which was something I had never really experienced before because I had been under the influence of alcohol when I had flirted and during the weekends back then. The difference between my situation and that of a sober teenager was that I had a child and lots of responsibilities.

I had to try to explain this to my little girl as best I could.

"Honey. It's totally mad to be in love. The doctors even call infatuation a disease. I know I talk about him a lot and think about him too. You do notice that I'm away in dreamland, don't you?"

"Oh, really?!!! I know, Mom, you're far, far gone!" She shook her head.

"It will get better. Just stay strong, my child! I will get back to normal – believe me! Luckily, you do know that

I love you all the time. Right?!!" She told me later that she did feel left out.

Luckily, she adored her "Plastic Daddy", as she called him, and they had lots of fun together. I suspect that they developed a deeper relationship thanks to me being so disconnected from the real world for a year, or maybe more.

Both Emma and I are very happy that we were invited to see "The Smurfs" in 3D. My feelings still tingle at the sight of him now, in this year 2016 and I hope that I always remember to tell him how much I appreciate having him in our little family.

Emma has gotten her own chapter in this book and my four siblings and I are joyously reunited. The larger family were out of the picture for many years but I have met most of them again now and they have been careful but always welcomed me with open arms. This was something I hadn't expected.

A whole generation of life with celebrations, children, people who have passed away, hardships and all kinds of family matters have transpired and I haven't been there to take part. Instead, I have been the one to bring sorrow and worry to them all. I am so thankful that we have each other today and I try to be as active as I can in seeing these loved ones.

My parents were very hurt and scared for me during those horrible years. For their wounds to heal has been more complicated. The resignation they had almost come to terms with concerning my drawn-out suicidal addiction had brought each of them to their own personal trauma. This, blended with the guilt they have felt, has brought them a lot of pain.

I understood that it would be difficult to win either of my parents' trust back. Their memories and the idea of the life we ought to have shared had caused deep sorrow and affected the paths their lives had taken.

My mother lived abroad until I was 18 and for long periods when it suited me to have her in my life, her everyday existence was weighed down by my manipulations and the obvious deranged mental state I was in from my alcohol abuse. She had to see first-hand how broken I was mentally and physically during the years I lived in Gothenburg. This was beyond painful for her.

Then, after I quit using alcohol and other drugs, she was there as a fantastic supporter through my recovery. I could always call her. She made sure that Emma and I got to travel, go to funfairs together and spend wonderful summer vacations with her on the archipelago of the Swedish west coast. Emma's musical talent and her love for water sports have been made possible largely thanks to her grandmother's support.

Now I have lost my mother to cancer, or rather to the harsh treatments which wore her organs down. I feel gratitude for the eight years of close contact we got to have and how our relationship grew in those sober years I was able to share with her. I know that she also valued every day of my sobriety.

My father and I see each other at least twice a year when Emma and I visit him in the unbelievably beautiful landscape of Dalarna in central of Sweden. He lives there with his sweetheart: they are still a happy, loving couple. Our relationship is growing stronger by the day. He moved back to Sweden in 2009 after a life abroad. This means that we are on a relatively new journey of getting to know each other. He was spared from seeing me when I was close to perishing from the disease of addiction. The most important thing I can do to make amends to him is to continue to take care of my recovery.

He has listened to my story of how I live my life today. He has understood the difficulties that parents in our time and before have had in understanding how a child follows the insane impulses of addiction. He has befriended the fact that humanity is still new to the idea that recovery from addiction is actually possible and that in the future it will be common knowledge. This has been an important mission for me in making my amends to him. It has helped him handle his guilt.

He has been to some of my talks in Sweden and has spoken to other people who have had the same experience as him. He has told me these conversations have been important for his making peace with himself. He also finds comfort in knowing that I am a determined and disciplined person. He believes me when I say that I have decided to take my recovery seriously. That I always remember the ruthless person I become with alcohol in my system. He sees that I do anything and everything not to be the one to relapse into that disordered insanity again.

The wealth in having these bonds, these sincere relationships, was a fortune I could never even have touched on picturing as long as I had the drug in my life. Then, I couldn't consciously allow myself to care what anyone else thought of me or whether or not they missed me. That was what I told myself. Anyone who expressed concern for my wellbeing was only trying to hinder me from my "freedom" to use my mind-altering substances and was therefore the enemy.

Looking back on memories of the times when I reacted to these kinds of expressions of love from my family and other people, it appears as deranged as it was. I literally hissed at their heartfelt advice about my safety, converting them into the threat to my wellbeing. That is the simple description of addiction. Completely life-defying insanity.

The thankfulness I feel toward being liberated from using alcohol or any other type of drug is immeasurable. Finally, I can have these loved ones in my life. My decision to maintain my zero tolerance for any type of buzz is written in love, directed toward myself and my relationships.

What my family and I need to be aware of is that love is not co-dependency. Love is healthy boundaries towards what is acceptable in one's own and others' behaviour. Giving something without considering what it could be used for is not always beneficial for the receiver.

I cherish the valuable moments where I am with and talk to others and, with thinking affirming thoughts and taking action to inspire courage, this works out quite well. To finally feel undiluted joy and intimacy with others is priceless.

The fact that I have begun to value my life is clear because, finally, I set healthy boundaries toward myself as well as to my fellow humans. I dare to face conflicts as well as being able to back down and review my own shortcomings. To me, these factors have proven themselves to be huge parts of my belonging. I get better at seeing how it is alright for me to behave with others and how it isn't. Through this, I also learn what I accept others doing to me, to Emma or other people, and what

I do not accept.

My fiancé once commented that I sounded very scornful and angry sometimes when I corrected Emma.

"I know that you aren't a mean person, but you sound very mad. She gets really sad when you do that, you know."

Before my recovery, I would have asked him to get out and never come back, but now I realised that what he said had some truth in it and that he meant well. I appreciated that he had such faith in our relationship that he dared bring this up with me. Since then, I have been able to act differently, or at least stop myself and if I don't see myself in time I can go back to tell Emma that I have behaved unforgivably.

I have people around me whom I love and who love me back.

Having fun is also something I have found to be very important. A life-affirming need. To dance, to play and joke around, to have hobbies and enjoy myself with others. To party, in other words!

The day-to-day sharing with others is exquisite. To meet people and share a moment of humanity through an unexpected kindness, a sudden spontaneous act of coming together to help another, to suddenly be aware of all the smiling and laughing in the streets and join in – these are acts which move me as deeply when they come from myself as from someone else.

After having lived like this for a decade, having seen this connection happen between humans, I can truly say that love is the greatest power of all.

To live in healthy relationships with people around me is the most important thing to me. To think I was that disconnected! To be present has brought me a life I had never been able to even dream of before. The jovial nightly dreams with me and the characters in "Friends" fade in comparison with the real deal. The pure joy I can share with another person is breath-taking!

Fellowship gives a deep resonance in my being that no dreamt or intoxicated state of mind can imitate.

The winning recipe for my new life is to daily refresh my ability to keep an appreciation of others, attracting me to having relationships. To love to be with others and, if need be, to allow for acceptance and courage to guide me in my everyday adventures of meeting people.

The emotional tides which occur in sober interactions with others, those inner tornados that sometimes appear to threaten my very sanity, are in fact the richness of having a real life. The times spent with other people are the memories I will sit savouring in my rocking chair during the autumn of my life.

To me, the people who value fellowship, who work at having well-functioning relationships with their fellow human beings, are the genuine nobles of this world. The only true upper class. They are the ones with actual fortunes to show for their lives. People sharing priceless resources with their values validated through their actions.

I look up to such values which are the solid foundations I aspire to build my life on.

Natural, honest and loving relationships in life are the most precious gift of all.

My desire is to always keep my senses open and sober, because then I have the opportunity to experience the sweetest of sounds, that ringing bell of belonging – this marvellous echo of love resounding in the depths of my spirit.

Spiritual Matters

If I have ever written anything personal about the way I live my life, my way of viewing things, this will be that chapter. I hope you, Dear Reader, keep this in mind when you read the reflections on the next few pages. This is my story, these are my personal beliefs. The way I ponder spiritual matters. To me, there are no rights and no wrongs in these questions. To each his or her own and, as always, as long as that way doesn't harm anyone else.

Throughout my life, I have nurtured numerous opinions about how human beings ought to treat each other. Theories flowed freely about how no-one else was able to manage treating each other, and foremost myself, humanely.

I harboured a strong hatred toward the co-hell-ision of mankind:

"Earth's ruling capitalist dictators who aren't intelligent enough to manage our planet. A dictatorship which a duped humanity allows and supports in the destruction and depleting of our world's labours and resources. The people of our planet are blinded by the worship of those who hoard money, suffocating their spirit at the altars of these superficial, mindless idols whom they cherish".

I stood firm, keeping myself apart from that whole mess. Or so I thought.

When I began to recover, I suddenly wanted nothing else but to be a part of society. The wonders of the coalition of man became stronger than the repulsion I had had toward the co-hell-ision.

To be included in the humanity became my daydream. Suddenly, I became aware of the fact that "normal" people were unique, good-hearted souls with dreams and goals, flaws and genius, just like me.

My worn-out role as an outsider had finally revealed its true goals and nature – its only purpose had been seeking the death of every part of me that was humane. In a flash of insight, the cornerstones of my accusations became crystal clear, I had been telling the tale of what I had actually been doing. The destruction of all that was delicate and living was what I had been doing.

I was a partaker in the destruction I loathed.

Now the will to live harboured itself in me and whatever reservations I might have, I would overcome them. To live a full life, I would be on a life-spanning quest in seeking to manage my existence to the best of my ability. To live with love and respect for others as well as for myself.

A question simmered inside though. I had now begun to sail the waters of a world I had hated. Was it even possible for me to align with it? How would I keep the love in my heart for this journey and how would I make this affection stay fresh?

As soon as my thoughts went to the faults of others and the abomination of the planet's disorderly state, I became physically nauseous. That type of reasoning was too coupled with my old way of thinking. Observing the powerful physical reactions these thundering chains of thought brought me, I guessed that the nausea sprang from subconscious associations with the decades I'd lived in drugged mental confusion. Reminders of my isolation.

So, there was a way for me to manage living without lapsing into the old ways of pointing fingers and judging others. I needed to keep the focus on my own actions, as best as I could, instead. As long as the surrounding world posed no threat to me or anyone else, I would practise letting people take responsibility for their own actions.

From having lived in a world where everything had been about fending off responsibility, I suddenly sought to make a complete turnaround.

In my first book, 'I Only Wanted to Dance', I use the word God. My ambition in writing this chapter is to use that word as little as possible, because naming the all-encompassing presence I believe in might associate this power with too many religious dogmas.

I actually don't have a fixed image of my God. Not even for myself.

To make this read easier, as well as the writing of it for that matter, I would like to clarify a few things:

I am not a member of any organisation that has anything to do with spiritual points of view.

I have read spiritual and religious literature and I attended spiritual talks when I was younger. Nowadays I rarely do, but it does happen.

I believe that I, everyone else and absolutely everything is in God - that is my truth.

A description of this power and my communication with it is difficult because I don't have an image of a specific entity or any out-lined ritual to follow. I have a sensation of being a part of an unlimited, loving power.

Sometimes, I search out that power by listening inwards, tuning to the peaceful serenity of my innermost chamber. Then I experience complete and undemanding affection. A power that only wants me to know that I am loved.

How then will I be able to write about spiritual matters if I don't mean to go into deep personal theories, of imaginings of my God? Well, this is not a problem because I view spirituality as a most practical matter.

Throughout my life, I have always been drawn to looking inward, but under the influence of alcohol and other drugs I experienced that my connection to that pure loving core became obscured. Whatever came out when I was in a chemical state was something fabricated – not naturally experienced.

I wasn't able to create. I tried but that which came out on paper was feigned. How could I write of beauty when I was polluting my body with poison?

I had the same feeling toward my creations back then as I got when meeting children if I was intoxicated – there was something fake in the air. I wasn't in actual contact with them because my true self was subdued by mind-altering substances.

I tried to say that drugs heightened and enhanced something that already existed within me but I can see today that, in comparison to creating while sober, what I wrote then was trivial. Closed off from my clean nature as a human being.

A lot of what went on those days was me talking, scribbling and theorising a lot about what I would and could do. Putting the world to rights, always feeling very enlightened under the influence of alcohol. But in actuality, I did nothing but express myself. Nothing that made anything grow. Not inside me nor in a way that would inspire anyone else. Those endless trains of thought, chains of "logic" without any grounding in actual experience and therefore of no substance or practical use to anybody.

Today I walk a different trail, I turn over soil and I plant seeds which often truly grow.

Without a doubt, the most thrilling and daring adventure is looking at how I behave. I need to put energy into how I live this life. Daily.

Focusing on my own actions has become one of the greatest reliefs I have ever experienced. At the same time, it is the one trait that can make me honestly make plans to take off to that deserted island where I'll have only myself in mind. But plans don't mean anything if I don't act on them. And I don't. I stay and pray to be a responsible person, then I spring into action on that desire. That's when I gain the wealth of being a fellow human being.

As a human among other humans, I do have a world surrounding me to take care of. I find that it is very important to have moral obligations that I can act on in the long run. Only complying with other people's whims, a swirling leaf with no values of my own, would destroy my self-worth. At times, complying is necessary in relationships. Then I try to weigh up whether my actions would respect my integrity and my values before agreeing with the person I'm supposed to cooperate with. My choice of action needs to have a solid foundation within me.

To be perceptive is one of the values I desire to have in the foreground. To be sensitive to what promotes life and co-existence is what helps me to co-relate. That virtue doesn't just pop up because I wish for it. I practice keeping an open-mind, being a perpetuum mobile in reclaiming the here and now. Observing what is going on in the moment, acting considerately with the greatest amount of integrity and the most caring boundaries that I can.

Boundaries are love. This is something very important which I need to consider when deciding whether my behaviour is acceptable. When I am able to set standards concerning my own actions, I notice that I am able to set boundaries for others in a way that I can stand up for, without being resentful. To me, this is loving spirituality in practice.

In my perspective towards caring about another person, I admire humane qualities in them which seem to occur when the emotional and intellectual planes are balanced. When this balance occurs, I can sense a pure intelligence. An intelligence with an all-including power greater than anything I have experienced before.

To me, the utmost meanings of intelligence, of being educated in life, of possessing essential attributes, have crystallized themselves into being humane, loving qualities. Abundant resources I can use and act on in any situation I face. Qualities that are eternally valid. The ones I use when being in the midst of the wonder of life with other people.

Our schools teach us varying subjects, many of which I need to use to support myself and that teach me to manage the resources at my disposal. Depending on which personal talents I have, these schools let me acquire what I need in that area of an occupation in life. Those are quite basic, intellectual functions which I dearly need to make the world I live in develop in a material sense.

To develop my humane qualities is more of what I regard as becoming an intelligent being. That type of education gives me the valuable tools needed to lead a life that holds wealth beyond mere survival. The inner resources that make my being grow rich.

So, to me, being intellectual is not the same thing as being intelligent. I am repeating myself, I know, but it is so very important to remind myself of this - when humane care and intellect meet, intelligence seems to spring forth. Resulting in actions of love.

Love being the greatest gift of all.

The two classic spiritual actions of prayer and meditation are a natural part of my everyday existence. The way I practice them though is very different from my earlier fixed ideas of how these most practical practices ought to be performed. I view my prayer and meditation as a mental out- and input. I will do my best to try and explain how I go about such a personal matter to make it work best for me.

Picture this if you will.

I come to a town I've never been to before and I need to find my way to the postoffice. I approach someone and ask the way. The question is put to this person from a frame of mind that is completely emptied, focused on the answer.

If I were to stand opposite the person who is answering me and at the same time keep on thinking:

"Well now she is going to say -

'Turn left here, then take a right and after 150 metres knock on the fourth door in the yellow house'

- then I would never hear the answer. I would never reach what I was trying to find. Instead, I empty my mind and wait to be guided by the answer I will be given.

In this example, the question is the prayer and the listening is the meditation. I do this several times a day. It can be anything from existential queries to finding answers to Emma's wonderings. From how to aid a fellow human being to which way to turn on my leisurely stroll through Malmö. The wonderings of the day-to-day issues of life.

I need to be like an atom that needs output and input

with the all-encompassing forces of the universe to make sense.

When I manage to keep an open mind, I find answers to my questions. It can take time or be quite instantaneous. Often I get solutions that I didn't have an inkling about before. This frame of mind makes me perceptive to my inner voice and also to other people, who are often the deliverers of answers to my spiritual queries. The idea to be open to intuitive ideas as well as to human advice and findings.

Sometimes I also get input and angles from media. A song lifting me up on a difficult day with its lyrics of love, the beauty of our planet or breath-taking adventures. Or, as once happened, on a day when I suspected my parenting had hit a new low, the hero in a TV-series gave invaluable and comforting advice to a worried parent.

Talk-show hosts and guests and reality-shows. I recall watching a dangerous group hike on Discovery where people had to trudge through really hard conditions. After a few days explosive arguments turned rather ugly, but finally even the most hard-headed participants found their willingness to resolve matters, and it all ended in very honest showdowns of feelings.

Then there is the internet where I can follow the lives of others and how they manage, how their communities work or, for that matter, don't work for its citizens.

All the countless things I can reflect on and get a global feel for.

How much the Earth has shrunk! How much more accessible it has become to us all. How people all over our planet can get together and inspire one another to love our world.

The internet is most enriching in my searches on practical matters around spiritual growth.

I am truly grateful and feel that my hope and trust for evolutionary progress both for myself and the world around me will come to pass. I believe that much of the expansion of human intelligence will happen thanks to the internet because the destructive and egocentric forces will have a much harder time covering their tracks these days.

For me, the media is an important fuel for keeping my spirit burning. Important for me to keep on believing in our species. To experience being among so many other people who love and care for our Earth.

I would be clueless if I didn't let go and allow something or someone other than my self-centred points of view steer me. Again like the atom needing others to create something more than its lone self.

Meditation and prayer as I perceive them are what give me the fuel which carries me through life. Not bound to rituals and steadily going forward. Integrated in how I function in relation to the world around me.

In my day-to-day routine this "clear mind" approach gives my mind space for noticing gut-feelings. For hearing what people say. An inner compass that points to what might be appropriate. I have countless examples of successfully getting through trials in my relationships and in my parental role thanks to prayer and meditation. Being open to advice instead of struggling alone. To be a listener, to talk to people and then weighing up what I sense might be a valuable course of action.

To leave a question open seems to lure ideas to the light, scooped out of a bottomless well that I would have been shut off from if I had let my instinctive reaction of excessive brooding take over my brain. A tendency I have for brainstorming drowns out the more subtle solutions and ideas. But it's remarkable that focusing on not having an inkling can become the resource that brings about such amazing life-quality. How it works is truly mysterious – but it does. Sooner or later.

As much as I can, I avoid praying that someone or something will suit the way I would prefer them to be. Rather I pray for guidance. To be given the opportunity to see how everyday things can be handled in the most loving way. The most loving way doesn't necessarily mean that I personally benefit from it. That truly isn't often the guidance I get. But it doesn't mean complying with harmful suggestions either.

To reflect and assess is the kind of meditation that works best for me. I use this tool in the here and now. At the beginning of my recovery I practiced more disciplined methods and I still do sometimes when I need more time, maybe to relieve stress. Then I can find a place where I can be more focused on serenity. Though for the most part I have presence in the moment, observing how I experience present situations and how I act. Since my concentration constantly flows, there is always an ongoing process of reclaiming the here and now.

I have noticed that to be present is a talent that comes with practice. Because my spontaneous reaction is to move the focus to another time or thing or to somewhere or someone else, this is an active process.

To me, this is communicating with my God. I view everything as being of this loving power and I can always lean on this power while doing my best to live a qualitative and healthy life.

Sometimes, I think that without spirituality and listening for guidance, I would have caused my family to crash a long time ago.

Arguments are common in our household. Thankfully, I understand that my truth isn't always another person's truth. So we put forward our cases. In some issues I am the grown-up and there is no room for debate. In others, I might need to re-evaluate my decisions. Emma does not have a compliant personality. I am not a pliant parent either. Neither is her "Plastic Daddy". Talks of having acted without concern for another's integrity and feelings are common issues. I am glad that we dare to argue!

When I am tired and Emma is having a tough day, this is always a wonderful opportunity to weigh the gut feeling of different ways to handle the present. One solution might be to rest because my recuperation can be what benefits the both of us. The other solution could be that this might be a situation where she is in dire need of talking to me, and that her need to air what is going on outweighs the need for a rested parent.

Being perfect is, thankfully, impossible. The need to have an inner desire to let love stand in the foreground in all areas of life seems to be what gives strength to perceptiveness in a situation like this. I have noticed that simply having this spiritual loving focus in the foreground makes wonders happen in the daily routine of being.

If the decision made is that Emma will wait or that her need for me postpones my rest for half an hour isn't really the issue here. The point I want to make is that in the long run, the outcome of whatever we end up doing seems to result in us being able to keep an evolving, keeping mutual respect. These kinds of everyday situations often resolve themselves for the better in the end, when a desire for love is what is underlining the process.

For the most part, that is it...

It would be boring to be perfect!

The way things turn out thanks to the reliance I have on being guided is sometimes a bit freakishly supernatural. I am the type of person who appreciates that one plus one factually does equal two. I often get caught off guard when attention to spiritual guidance is clearly what helps me the most in my development as a person. It is also creepily clear how my attention to spiritual principles affects my relationships with people around me.

I don't get involved in discussions about the existence of this invisible power nor whether courses of events are just destiny or whether I can influence them. Because really, who knows?!

The only thing that is certain is that yes is yes and no is no.

When a situation out of my control occurs, I am the one who decides how I will go about tackling this and then I follow my intuition, my gut feelings.

To try to elaborate on these matters would just be speculation. Of course I wonder. Who doesn't? But I let these questions go out in prayer and meditation. I think I believe in endless theories on the subject and, at the same time, none.

As the saying goes - "God works in mysterious ways".

What I am sure of is, that ever since I became sober, existing with a mind unclouded by drugs, the spiritual connection I experience has grown stronger and become a most tangible and very real part of my life.

I was on my way home one afternoon and I was close to feeling completely depleted. I had my course set for heading straight home. I was so beat that my head was swimming in a way that maybe only burnt-out people can understand.

As I approached on the walkway which would lead to the nearest route to our house, an incessant pull began urging me to go straight on instead, into Triangeln, a shopping mall close to my home. Close but still a few minutes off my course and I had absolutely no errands to run there. The pull was so strong I actually began debating in my head.

"I'm not going in there! Why in all the world should go in there!? I am tired – I have to go home!"

"No, you don't", this strong pull was almost physical. In my worn-out state, I gave in and thought that I might as well just go through the mall to get this urge to simmer down. I hadn't felt such a strong inner pressure before. At least not when I was so bent on going home.

I walked through, with my head down, looking at the floor. Then suddenly I heard them. My sister, her children and husband. I looked up and there was my brother who I hadn't seen in ages and who wouldn't be caught dead in a shopping centre and they were all in the company of an old family friend. My sister and her family didn't live in Malmö at the time and I was quite new to recovery so they hadn't gotten into the habit of calling me when they gathered.

The pure joy they all showed when they suddenly and spontaneously had me in their midst was a huge band-aid for all of us in the process of re-integrating me in the family. Then they all asked the others who had been the one to call me. They were all just meeting in the mall because the daughter had to get some little thing quickly, then they would be off to where their actual destination was.

Nowadays, I hardly reflect on it when these kinds of things happen because they often do. Not as strongly as that time though because I was really, really dead on my feet that day and would not in a million years have gone out of my way without that nagging gut feeling pulling me in the "wrong" direction.

Maybe we have some kind of inbuilt radar like some other animals are suspected to have, maybe I could smell them or maybe a team of angels are bustling about in the air all around humanity guiding us.

I wouldn't know. But admittedly, this is a part of my daily life that I do find a bit spooky, for sure!

My most and immensely-valued spiritual principles are those of gratitude, hope and trust. Companions as important as the air I breathe on the trail of life. Without them, I am easily lost in blinding self-absorption such as greed, misery and aversion.

These are the spiritual qualities that are the spontaneous base for my daily outlook. When I get caught in troubled situations and seem to get nowhere with a disgruntled state of mind, I actively search these three out. I know that whatever I am facing, I will find it easier to turn things around when I have at least one of the three to lean on.

As my doctor told me about people who have survived any deadly disease or life-threatening accident, these three companions often become a part of living for that person. Being an addict and having found recovery after having survived the suicidal and mentally confused disease of addiction, I always have gratitude, hope and trust comforting me deep inside. I only need to give a little bit extra focus to give them a chance to surface, if they have sunk too deep.

I will attempt to give at least a small insight into what these spiritual qualities mean to me. Spirituality has a lot to do with my ability to be present. These following examples are attempts to describe what practical spirituality means to me.

Gratitude.

When I'm on my bike, in the windy coastal town of Malmö, struggling with the gusts, I often bear a strong grudge, which at that moment is the strongest ingredient in the spectre of my feelings.

The simplest way to let gratitude win over that resenting attitude is to take hold of the now. Look up, silence my discontent by taking in the surroundings and soaking up the wonderful miracle of life around me. The tiniest spring flower or the miracle of rain, a feeling of sudden appreciation for the wondrous invention of the automobile driving by, smiling at the chattering pedestrians jumping to the side at the sound of my bicycle bell or to abruptly be made aware when someone suddenly shouts to warn me about an obstacle in the road. The little things.

When I left the hospital in the early morning after my mother had passed away in the night, the sun was shining on my face, on my tears, and the birds chirped their songs of busyness. I waved back to the bus driver who hailed me on the empty streets of Gothenburg. Even then, gratitude held my heart.

Being in the present, there is always dizzying proof of the miracle of humanity existing around me. The incredibly fantastic wonders of the human sphere. Life in the middle of the universe, the universe in the middle of life. Such presence lets gratitude spread like wildfire in my senses. A tingle of the spirit at being in the midst of the sheer miracle of us all.

Hope.

I dive into it and it is the fresh air of my soul. The sense of there always being something I can do to lift myself up.

To remind myself of the days I existed with a closed, harried mind sometimes helps me when hope is scarce. If I can't muster it alone, I only have to get myself somewhere to meet someone. To share a moment with Emma, to smile and talk to the lady in the elevator, to give a spark of eye-contact to a stranger. Often simple actions like these are enough to ignite hope within. Already in that first moment of contact, hope gets brighter.

A fire in the spirit at acting on what is doable.

Trust.

What a wonderful thing to have carry me. It is also, if not most of all, bound to what I actually do. Trust is where the practical spirituality reaches its peak. I am trustworthy when I do the things I talk about.

The same goes for my trusting others. I can trust a fellow human when I see the person doing what she said she would do.

I have proof that I can live a life in which I know where I stand. Before, I tried to trust promises, wishes and dreams. Now that actions are what I trust, life is suddenly real.

Anchored by the fact that yes is yes and no is no.

This is my personal spirituality.

Outer circumstances always directed my bearings before. If the liquor store was open, if someone reacted as I wanted them to and so on. Now I find it makes me more and more uncomfortable when I lay my happiness on something outside of my spirit. But I do it. Of course. This is a most human thing to do. And then, of course, I get an empty feeling when the ride is over. That is when I need to remember to remember that I am always in alignment with the here and now even if I forget it for a while. Gratitude, hope and trust embrace me from within again and contentment fills up the emptiness. At least until the next time the shiny, glistening promise of a glorious venture sends me galloping off into the promising horizon.

The difference between these adventures and the addictive destructive patterns is that my flights are manageable today and, most importantly, they aren't a threat to my life or to the safety of the people around me.

I've had the opportunity to try a great variety of escape routes since 2006. Among others, I've tried to work myself to fulfilment, I chased money, hunted prestige in society, tried neighbourhood snobbery and competitiveness, fixing other people, food-binging, exercise, gambling - with and without money (oh, the lure of Facebook games) and sugar, which I still get blinded by on and off.

I've even sniffed around the edges of different spiritual elitisms, fleeing into an "I have found the true path"-notion of the "chosen ones".

There is always something new around the next corner. Sometimes, I turn back to one or the other of the above, even if they have let me down time and time again, despite knowing that they are deceiving me with their "Marlboro-man promises" of guaranteed satisfaction.

The void I am trying to fill never seems to get enough of all this stuffing. I usually try until I suddenly stand there, observing that dissatisfaction has taken over my sanity again. The craze of self-centredness shouting that I deserve more and better. Once again I remember that there is something that always works, and then I re-align with the present, stuffing the void with love from within. Remembering that these outside, seemingly saviour-bright obsessions always bring emptiness and that their promises are always temporary and fleeting delusions of satisfaction. The love from within is always there if I search it out. Always offering a sense of belonging, solace and hope.

Adventures are a huge part of being human and I get more experience with every new escapade.

As long as it isn't alcohol, other drugs, gambling, relationships or anything else through which I can violate myself or others by galloping straight into them, it's okay. I catch myself in the act and then there is always the safe embrace of my loving God to rest within, the selfless love that I am always a part of.

Today, I choose to act on decisions that promote living life according to simple spiritual principles. These are practical, active choices, always bearing the nourishment I need for the daily journey on the turbulent sea of existence.

I live a thankful life today. Who would have guessed?

Surely, the future holds countless moments for retaking the observation of the present. It is enjoyable to escape a little in dreams, longing and searching.

A desirable path for me is to keep something of a balanced adventure.

The most important thing I had to do to begin with was to get over my old conception of spiritual matters being tied to religious dogma. It was then, and only then, that I found a way to spring into action.

The place I have on Earth is wonderful because each day I create a life I can stand up for, always leaning on guidance, aligning with my loving God. As long as I do my best, I am exactly where I am supposed to be.

Spirituality in practice.

My desire is to continue being responsible for my actions, to be of aid to others and practice loving qualities, because this is what I understand to be a fruitful way of life.

Part Two

Memories, the Present and Desires

Am I One and All?

I'm sitting looking inward. The first part of this book is written. When I go through the script in my mind, there is no longer anything which prays to be told, nothing that scratches at the surface, waiting to be let out.

It is done.

Six years have passed since I began tapping away at the keyboard, urged by an inner fire to share this dance I am in with life. Telling of bringing light into a sphere where darkness had ruled so cruelly.

Telling of hope and the joy of being a part of something.

How can I possibly go on with writing this last part? The one to bring together the description of the importance of me being vigilant and keeping my death-defying power steadily flowing within? Will I find the words to describe the love for life that I feel? Will anyone understand?

The sun is hot and the questions rock me in the depths of my wicker chair. There, in the borderlands of deep relaxation, where serenity lives, it wakes me. In a moment of clarity I see it. The way to write unfolds itself as if the story had its own life.

But how could I possibly write it like that?

I look around inside, but there I can only find the one way to round this up. It is as if shutters have been put up against any other way to transcribe this finale. What I get when I observe inward and forward is simply and without detours exactly what will be told in these next few pages. It is all that I see. As if it were already written.

From the deepest well of my being, I hereby express all honour for life, for passion toward all that is humane and speaks to tender management for the Earth, our birthplace and home.

Now I will carefully step out into the twirling swirls of the dance of life.

Dear Reader! May I?

Memories

What do I do with them, all these memories?

Childhood's inescapability. Simply being in an atmosphere of existence.

The years that followed, years of insanity and ruthlessness, in constant flight without a flicker of presence.

To the new, the now, a fifth of my life, with memories woven from pure emotion, sorrow and joy in tumultuous harmony, a constant fuelling of the love for life, that which carries me through all things.

My memories, which only I can care for. Which only I can cherish. Which only I can share. I will do this in the care of the power that loves me, knows all of me and only ever wants what is best for me.

The longing for the times when the child was its own and tied only to itself. Can I claim that that freedom has passed? Can I belong to it, to that unchained existence, even as a responsible adult now dealing with the world around me?

How much can I bear to remember, knowing that I need to make amends?

Are there memories that are too painful, too brimming with regret that they become obstacles in my path?

Can I observe them? Can I be one with them? To be one with that which I did? That which caused others harm and more than that.

Can I measure the wealth of the memories since the 11th of March 2006?

Is there any way I could possibly share even an ounce of the vitality I have been dealt, a thousandth of the trust I experience, give even an inkling of the love that I experience for my being?

I will tell some of it all. Through these short bursts that came to me in my wicker chair I might find some answers to my questions, maybe an idea as to why I ever wrote these books.

Memories, the present and desires – can I be one and all?

*

First under each title is a memory from childhood.
Second comes recollections from my addictive years.

Third, I write about experiences I've had the privilege of going through in my recovery.

You are welcome, Dear Reader, to journey with me through these occasions that somehow stood out in the serenest of moments in my wicker chair while contemplating what was left to tell.

*

Movement Outdoors

The feeling of the untouched forest feeling me walking through it. So Ångermanlandish, so chock-full of life and berries.

I followed a thin path. I, the smallest of children, helped by keeping it tread down. I walked alone, on and on, undivided with the Earth, touched only by sudden prickling.

The air I moved when moving. The density of it, thickly needle-scented, the rustling humidity. Life within life within life.

The hut came into view, fresh pine-branches adorned the little thing, well, rather it was huge, at two lengths of me. I knelt down and crawled inside. Alone, safe within the sturdy birch frame. Here I was at peace. Alive with its sound, movement and scent, the planet about me was breathing within my breathing.

Thoughts roamed of branches to replace, if the ground were to be made less bumpy, then a drink of lemonade from grandmother's hundred-year-old flask.

Contentment at being here.

*

The LSD was wearing off. There was some hash. I split it so it would last. The night was short but the time until there would be more alcohol was endless. The sky was less dark in its first light. From the cape the next cape made its appearance out of the foggy veils.

A hare. A fox. The cries of seabirds. Stones and bushes showing off fantastical shapes and colours creating fantastical shapes and colours revealing yet more, deeply unreal shapes and colours...

The body was reignited with the smoke which I held inside until nothing came out. The chemistry changed and the light crept forth, timely out of night.

Something came in a movement on the cape across the waters.

What was it? What moved like that? Not a hare. Not a fox. A wolf?

The cape on the other side of the waters from my cape suddenly didn't seem far away enough.

Whatever it was it moved on, with determined purpose.

Not a hare, not a fox – it knew too precisely where and how it was going. The strides, the motion gave it an approach without comparison. No wolf could compare to this predatory, goal-bent orientation.

I became the target. I was scared, my bones chilled.

What is it? Too fast. Too close - almost at the end of the cape now. My refuge next. Minutes away. I sat still. It hadn't spotted me. Yet.

Could I even hide from such a creature?

The light fell on something. Something stood out from its back. A stick. What animal carries a stick like that? Why would it?

It steered clear of a boulder, several steps ahead of it and then I saw the man. I saw how it ploughed through the cape. Took the parting path, away from me. Towards the parking lot. With his fishing gear.

Repelled and disgusted – as always by my kind.

The distance could never be far enough.

*

I wrote about writing.

I wrote of a time in a future. Of my child in her own room with a sleep-over friend.

Of a time of family, home and work.

In the background I hear a Midsummer song sung by the people in the field, children of all ages hooting, grown-ups mingling, many like me – having found their way out. Into freedom. Into the here and now.

The scent of newly-cut hay.

The swatting of gnats.

I sat by myself on a garden patio, looking out over the open landscape, needing space, longing, writing about my child, about our, my, vision.

All the love shared among the crowds around me almost soothed my missing of Emma. She was so far away, in a family that was another. Despite this, she was closer now than she had ever been, ever since her birth.

I was present, finally present.

Writing consoled me with its surging tale of happiness, of courage and contentment.

I could hear her, the whispers from the playroom.

I had the feel of my chair, sitting in a home, our home, in the cone of light from my desk lamp, seeing the text outlining.

A preview of my future in the completing of books.

Comfort and hope enveloped me at last. The others were dancing now, large rings around the maypole, and I rose. Walked along the path through the tall grass, to the people celebrating the most wonderful of feasts. I joined in with the movement, skipping along with the singing of the old songs, the tales of ripeness to come and of summers. That celebration of life, of light and abundant future harvests. The feast of the explosive force of bloom.

Gladdened by the children of others, soothing my sadness, knowing that many of their journeys resemble my own child's. That the parents are like me.

Smiling, undivided in the knowledge that my daughter was my daughter, and that our time was without question nearing its time. I celebrated the budding of our family.

*

Roofs

Flat roofs!

"Look, Titti! Flat roofs!"

The nanny smiled, nodding.

"Yes, it is strange, isn't it?" She stretched across me to see.

I didn't know what to believe. It was beige and narrow, that town below. Between the houses was a lot of junk. The plane flew low to make its stopover in Athens.

Flat roofs. What was a person to think about that?

Istanbul. People absolutely everywhere. A grande hotel for a few nights before going to my new home in Jordan. From the house in the outskirts of Gävle to here. To the bustle, the animals braying in the streets and the people, the shouting. There was a lot of shouting. It was as if all the children were being called in to supper. All at once. All the time.

But the strangest thing was those flat roofs. Absolutely. That was the deepest-felt acknowledgement of the fact that we were moving. The strangeness which sealed the adventure permanently.

I mean, really. Flat roofs?

*

24 years old and never before in such a huge concrete complex.

How many hundreds of flats could there be? How did one live here? A box in a box. The only answer I could befriend was temporarily. I could only cope with the thought of the answer having to be temporarily.

Temporarily became a while but there was the kick, and that was always new. Wasn't it?

The first syringe here. Yet another kick. Ruts were for cluts. The kicks had to be new. Missing out chased me, so where was the next new one? The next unique one? The rush that would be the one to complete me?

How could you live like this? I wasn't like anyone else. I lived on the surface. There, on the surface, the differences were huge. Bushes. Stairwells. Trains. Nothing like these flatlined boxes.

But I stayed. Temporarily.

New doses, mixtures and kinds. No kick like another.

Without being drunk you shrunk. Without a drink you shrink. Poor, fooled humanity. Shrunken, shrinking losers.

Missing out, hanging, too hungover, detesting life. Find the next new one. Surely the same old will be new. It will be fresh. Different now?

Re-evaluating what you do and don't do, just this once. Getting inside, making exceptions for the box. Concrete nouveau.

Filled up and most un-fresh. Where did it go, the uniqueness? Seeking, reeking with desperation.

Always new attempts at lifting tempers, filling days, stealing for the Christmas table.

In a box in a box under an enormous flat roof.
There my amazement withered further. There it was all beige and the junk was mine. Inside the temporary progressed towards the permanently dulled. There the whole world was flat. More so than any flat roof.

*

The water-jug held high, she flew about, my child, calling:

"Mother! Can I give it them? Those or these or what? Whoops! Spilt some..."

"That's fine. Great. Happy plants."

Distracted. Distraught. The view was fabulous! Past the flat roof, I could see Folkets Park, the People's Park, by our house. Beyond that, the southern boroughs of the city. Buildings scattered, mostly flat-roofed, like tiny boxes littered about by a giant. Gorgeously angular, of every colour, on display. The thought of the sun-chair I would put out on this roof if I lived here.

The neighbour's keys jingled. Me! With the neighbours' keys!

"We're going abroad for a few weeks. Would you mind watering our plants? If it isn't too much of a bother...?" The crash in my head! An uplifting crash. Yet again.

The week before there had been the matter of a few of the parents of Emma's classmates who had hurriedly turned away at the very sight of me. Their faces saying:

"Oh, no, not her again! That do-gooder class-mom. Do I have the money for the teacher's flower? Forgot. Again. Shit! Hope she didn't see me!"

Me representing conscientiousness!?

The week before that there had been something else and so it went now. Life and all. Always something new. The crashes that unexpectedly and joyously shook my whole being.

All under this flat roof. Our building enveloping these new memories of happiness and hope, strife and sorrow. Of life.

Confidences reverberating. This is what I am a part of now. I who lived out there before, between the roofs, shutting all of this out with all my might. I am now one with the world. Even with these, all of these very many flat roofs.

"Mother, can we go out there? Pleeease! Mother! I want to walk on the roof! Why are there rocks on it? Cool that it's flat so that no one gets them, those sharp little boulders in the head, don't you think?"

"Yes, darling one, isn't it? It's really cool with the flat roofs. Come on, let's climb out. Of course we dare. They're flat, aren't they?"

*

The Sea

Mother called me to the buffet. I took my little sister's hand and together we walked from the stern. The salon had a huge table in the middle, now decked with sausages, meat, chicken, potatoes, sauces, fruit and lots and lots of cookies.

"Not the cookies! First you eat food!"

Hm. I hadn't seen her standing there in the passageway. The yacht was huge. Yeah, yeah, okay. Food is not a problem. I love food.

It was wonderful to be under the Saudi sun. It felt different to the Jordanian one. Maybe just because I knew. I ate, forgot about the cookies when I heard loud hooting from the stern.

Tuna!

Little brother fought with the rod. No, no, no one was allowed to help him, the men winked and smiled at each other. Understanding. He was strong, the little man. The rod was almost aligned with the surface of the sea and the beast thrashed out there.

"Way to go!" I shouted, took off on my own adventure and went to see the skipper. He was the friend of the family, the one who had borrowed the King's yacht. I wanted to see the sonar. Please!

The days when we used the boat were long and delicious. I just couldn't get enough. Always asking when we were or could, that we must, really, really must, go out again.

Standing alone, scouting the choppy surface in the free winds. The boat and I, at one with the elements.

In and out of the sun. The food. The sonar. Above sharks and reefs. Exploring the luxurious ship.

Homeward, dusk. The sun glistening on the water, the gold of my life as always being the adventure, the sun mirroring the gleam of my soul.

Pure and raw experience! It was the most wondrous of days. Out there. At sea.

*

Seabergs. That's what the sailors called them. Huge mountains of sea. Despite her size, 280 metres from stern to bow, the waves were dangerously high for the ship. Seabergs de l'Océan Pacific, by Jove. I was fed up, tired and, as always, but never enough, drunk.

"Fucking old farts."

I dragged the black garbage bag out onto the deck. I was to throw it overboard. Here it was only a show for the coastguard, this rule of garbage disposal. Outside the territorial waters, out on the unguarded sea, we threw it all overboard. Environmental polluting, following orders from above.

"Fucking old farts!"

Yeah, yeah – done for the day. The crate of the carbonated gold of my life awaited. The food they could keep. Today like so many other days.

But first things first. The damn garbage over the railing.

Six o'clock in the evening and it was pitch black out. The spray from the lurching sea tasted salty and I tugged. Suddenly, at the bulwark and, oh shit, this was a rough sea if ever there had been one! In an instant I awoke from the resentful coma. Sailor-coma. A flake to the elements.

Inside my voice suddenly roared:

"OhMyGodGirl! What the fuck are you doing? One

harsher lurch and you'll be flying like a cotton-wad overboard! Hold on you crazy bitch! GodDamnIt!"

One hand for the heaving, one hand for myself, holding
onto the ship. The bag was devoured, swallowed like a
molecule of a flea-spit by the Seaberg.

Having participated in furthering the damnation of
the ecosystem and still alive, I soon sat with the beer
in my cabin.

Fed up, tired and as always, but never enough, drunk.

*

It never went "scratch", it only went full-stop.

Two heads swirled, astonishment filled the craft, two
pairs of wide eyes meeting.

Corners of mouths twitched in unison, freezing in the
stalest of Hollywood grins. Glances snuck to the shore,
sweeping the east-coast bay-side. No one had seen. No
one was hooting.

"Puuushhh", we hissed.

Paddles shoved against the rock, away came the canoe
and the frozen faces melted into guffaws, togetherness
that pushed us free.

"Hahaha – lucky no one saw us!!!" A cooperative victory over the elements.

This was one of the many trips we'd made to sea, my
beloved daughter and I.

Blekinge, east-coast Sweden, on our starboard side, and all the happier for it were we.

Off the sea-hidden rock we'd run aground on. Suddenly it had been there, in the middle of the water. Hardly even our fault, that. No holes in the bulk. So we paddled along, strengthened by pure gratitude. Me at the stern, the child at the bow.

Happy, until the current took us and the wind began sighing heavily.

Rough sea. Serious attempts at putting blame on the other paddler, squabbling about how, when and if we ought to have paddled or not...

Where did they come from, the current, the wind?

Both of us, close to tears.

I am the grown-up. Breathe. Shouting, sounding as calm as I could over the gusts.

"I am the one steering. We have to do it this way. Darling girl. Just you keep on paddling as fine as you are and we'll soon be ashore again. It wasn't okay for me to get angry like that. I got really scared, see."

She glared at me from under her bangs and nodded.

"Okay, mother. I'll just paddle. But you were very truly unfair!"

Don't answer back. No more fighting. Paddle and pray for serenity.

"Hey you! Gold of my life! We'll soon be there. You're fantastically strong!"

We were going to manage our tour on the open sea. Evening was coming upon us with promises of grilled food in the company of great friends and family. The man in our family was waiting for us on dry land somewhere.

I steered clear of the troubles and Emma paddled purposefully on. She really had muscle and focus, this little person!

Strengthened by working together, on fire from conquering the elements. The best boat ride I had ever been on!

This victory would soon be celebrated with everyone at the camp.

Party!!!

The Present

An observer of living in the middle of life.

To be in the moment. To watch what moves in my thought processes.

To let my yearning be a presence.

The now. Being here. Doing this.

Thanks to what I do in the now, my desires for the future can be realised. To be present aids me in making this effort less pretentious. Making life at the same time both practical and genuine.

When I used to gamble for money, even though the bets were tiny, I was unable to be present. Anything but attentive to what I deep-down desired to do with my life.

When I used drugs I put the promise of wellbeing into an illusion of a substance-fabricated state of mind.

When I talked about living adequately, enjoying life and being contented, I lay these qualities in the dreams of utopian, future existences, pictured from imagination, without any foundation in my actual daily life. Forgetting the wonder of the present, the changes I could make in the now.

What I had in reality was somehow secondary. I never saw that life was what was happening right then.

That was my life. That was of course in the now of then. The question was whether I was able to see it or not. Whether it was the past before I knew it.

When I dream today, I retake the moment, I wake up to the now and reap the fruits of hope.

Present. To the best of my ability.

Memories, the present, desires ... What could I be if neither one nor all?

*

I wake up to a new world. Every day. A world that peers back at me with curious eyes and a smile luring me with all its possibilities. The lines in the contours of this reality tell of a story and a perspective beyond my ability of understanding. At the same time, I am aligned with this being our, my and my species', story. Our universe and solar system's tale of human beings, living another day, being in existence.

A story I help to fill every day here on Earth. A fresh, unwritten sheet coloured with everything that makes me reverently breathe, walk and love, one step at a time. Co-existing on this magnificent planet with all its teeming forms of life. New beginnings.

The absolute wonder of being alive!

To sit in the square and be a tourist in my hometown.

To set my outlook afresh to what is there, in my sight. Open-mindedness to the new. With all my experience, all my memories, with all that I do and desire to achieve, this view is complete when it is set free.

From the viewpoint of a newcomer, the panorama settles into the soul as a lightly-sweetened, newly-pressed lemon-juice drunk from a frosted glass on a warm summer day. Fantastically freshening to the core.

An existence in clarity.

A complete belonging in our world.

Some say that looking through a child's eyes gives them the freshness I describe with my metaphor of the tourist, but to me childhood was never as liberated. Never as clear-sighted. Never adorned with the freedom that taking responsibility in adulthood gives me.

I prefer the observing mode of a tourist. I was never this untroubled as a child...

Troubles have always owned lots of space between my ears. I am beginning to learn about spotting this energy thief that I let thrive within me.

"Most of the things you fear will never happen!"

The words echo of truth inside. When I catch myself worrying I'm reminded of the leakage of power I am indulging in and then I take back the now. Reviewing the present as it is.

The wildly varying catastrophic messes I've envisioned evaporate after a moment of inner exercises. The dramatic focus ebbs out.

I have accepted that worry is a part of being human. Without tentacles outwards and inwards, the calculation of risk, we would probably never have survived as a species. The ego that so protectively safeguards us when we are in potentially life-threatening situations.

I believe this alertness is inbuilt within me, but I often react to it to an extremely disproportionate degree. To dangers which most times aren't there. With practice, I have gotten better at observing worry for the overblown trait that it is in our peaceful, modern society. Despite everything, the human race has actually never seen this little violence before. We are, as ever, evolving.

Another part of worry is when I need to plan for something. In the planning stage, this kind of worry is a positive drive which, in corresponding proportions, becomes a positive force.

A focus on the inner compass, the gut-feeling, is important to me when assessing whether a worry is legitimately based on logic or if it is undue and instead a factor which is hindering me.

Made-up worries are such a waste of my time! With being observant in the now of what I'm thinking and saying, what is going on between my ears, I have noticed that I free up more and more time. Being observant without analysing. Seeing myself in the moment.

I am the kind of person who watches, broods, plans and needs to find balance.

Now is the time I live in. Life on Earth is invaluable and I minimize time-wasting by focusing on what's real. When compulsions, which are quite disturbing thoughts, rage within me, I need to find an exit. I centre myself inwards to my core and search for a solution.

Catastrophic delusions probably come over me because of my unmanageable life in the past. Always calculating risks. These just spring out from old habits or instincts and have been something that I've needed to find a method for handling.

An example of this thief of presence is one of the tales that came to me in the wicker chair. A solution to an ordinary day-to-day problem begging to be told.

For a time, I had unnerving sensations when I was just about to fall asleep. I was overwhelmed by an inner surge that I was standing by the window on our, the ninth, floor and, out of nowhere I just fell out. Maybe the scene was that I was walking and tripped out, or just standing by the window and somehow slipped out of it. The fear pulled me out of my going to sleep phase and for a long while I would lay wide awake with the terror pounding inside.

Of course, I could see that falling out of a window from the ninth floor was a sound thing to be watchful of not doing. My overblown reaction to this natural caution was far from sound and my sleep pattern was disturbed by me having this dread haunting me every night. Despite understanding the logic of this, it didn't make the surge go away.

After many prayers and meditations, a solution finally came to me. When the falling and fright came upon me, I simply let myself fall and, half-way down, rushing toward the pavement, I would stretch out and fly. Like a bird I soared upwards, gliding over the rooftops, sailing across the sky of my city.

It took a lot of practice to do this but from the first time, the relief was huge. It does work. I have developed other scenarios for this particular scene. One of my favourites is the one where I turn into a ninja-warrior half-way down the building and break my fall by catching onto a windowsill or a brick with my fingertips, then erupt into leaps across the building's facade, swinging off balconies until I land on my feet in a great warrior pose, with the mandatory "Haiii-Ya!!!".

This method is also something I apply in other situations where illogical fears overwhelm me. When fears of Emma getting hurt suddenly flare up in my mind, I can imagine her turning into the soaring martial arts hero of the century.

To battle imagination with imagination has really proven itself to be a great relief in these moments of sudden catastrophic illusions capturing my sanity. As unlikely as it would be for me to just suddenly, haphazardly fall out of a window, it is just as unlikely that I would be able to fly. Nothing is too silly to use to reset your presence in the reality of now. Where my priceless life owns a rightful place.

Yet another example of how the gift of prayer and meditation carries me in searching out loving solutions to everyday problems.

I must say, it is most exciting to live these days. There is a lot going on. Right now!

*

To partake in the courage of living my life in the real world fills me with wonder and fuels a fiery lust for life every day.

So much in life is about courage. If not everything.

To summon courage in the here and now.

To dare to put words to that which moves me.

To dare to be available to others.

To dare to observe my desires for what they are.

To dare to be small.

To dare to love.

To dare not knowing.

To dare being simple.

To dare to see my fear, my inhibition, my shortcomings, my bravery, my spontaneity, my talents.

To dare to rejoice, hope, do the unknown, say that I behaved badly, say that I behaved wonderfully.

To dare to just be.

To dare to include everything in the present, without analysis.

To dare to let presence, stillness, be a platform.

To dare to observe the disturbance of constant thought processes.

To dare to trust that serenity generates fruitful chores.

To dare to be one with knowing that now is all that is real.

To dare to see this list being infinite and eternal.

Lifting a still desire to be allowed the courage to be freed from the incessant chatter, to silence the swirling words that separate me from what is really going on.

To retake the gift of capturing the moment.

Being the adventurer that I am.

Exploring on the pinpoint of living.

Looking inward with the eyes of a tourist.

Silently, in awe.

*

I awake to a world filled with possibility. I am a clean slate when I choose to be. I see the miracle and potential of humanity.

My love for us and the home of our species is limitless. The only acceptable fact is this love.

My heart aches for all I am willing to learn about setting strong boundaries for what is acceptable.

Evolving out of love for our kind and all living things.

I do what I can.

It is now that life happens.

*

I am sitting writing in the main town library of Malmö. Up on the third mezzanine, beside the five-storey tall glass wall. I see the same view as I did eight years ago when I was writing about this exact moment. I am fulfilling that cycle in this now.

The text I wrote then was about how I would be sitting here, being in the final words of a book. Filled with expectation, trepidation swirling inside. I feel now exactly what I felt then. I've kept that text in a drawer at home, looking at it to summon the courage to continue, and those words tell exactly of what I feel, right here, right now.

I am sitting writing with all my heart.

I prose on the life I live, the love I feel and the hope I carry.

Of that which I burn with. Of this, that is happening.

Of knowing that we are all worthy of conjuring up the courage to make each day as good as possible.

Of love being the greatest fuel of all.

The egocentricity of what is and what was is my responsibility. An obligation on an individual in evolution, to admit that which I desire to evolve beyond.

To see how courage in the now carries me to do things differently is to see further than the self-centred fear and to finally grow up as a human being.

What a liberating existence! What wealth! What a wonderful world we live in!

Desires

My foremost desire is to stay. Stay living.

Consciously living.

Taking part without diluting reality with mind-altering substances.

Staying present, whatever comes to pass.

To be able to experience happiness from the heart.

To be sad from the depths of my sorrow.

To enjoy pure intimacy when I am near another person.

To be responsible for my life, as part of humanity, as one in all.

An individual partaker in all matters.

I desire to always remember where I come from.

I desire to keep an open mind every day.

I desire to choose to make each day a valuable one.

When I take responsibility, the love for life comes to me and stays.

I desire to keep living like this.

In the ever-new.

To be the one I, deep down, always wished I was.

To aspire to be one I desire to be.

To love the one I am and hence to know to love another.

To remember to pray for courage despite my shortcomings.

To remember to pray for being in evolution.

To continuously pray for being an asset.

Actually, it can all be said in one simple sentence:

I desire to keep on praying to remember that love has always been, always is and always will be the greatest power of all.

***

Memories, the present and desires.

Yes.

I am one and all.

In the Backwashes of a Dream

I pushed my feet down. My arms went like pistons. The black water in the gentrified docks outside glittered, rippling with silver streaks. The grip of the night's dream was slowly, too slowly, loosening its hold on my being. All I could do was wait it out and push harder, focusing my grip on the handles of the cross-trainer. Focused on the water beyond the window-glass wall in front of me.

Suddenly, the deadened sensation lifted, I hadn't even been aware it was there. Sensations surfaced and softly I was awoken to consciousness.

"Oh, shit!" My whole being resounded. "Oh, shit! So that was it. What I missed."

Close to tears in an instant.

*

I was alone at the table under a roofed picnic area in the park. I was terribly aged inside but looking good. As always, looking good. The beer half-empty in my hand. The thoughts of whether there was someone else coming or whether I was going to be able to have the whole crate to myself. Many concerns about the crate which I had spent long and cumbersome hours fixing. I had placed a few cans in a bag in the bushes in case anyone showed up to claim their share.

My clothes were clean and well-suited for the time and place. There was something erratic about the whole picture though, but I couldn't put my finger on it. I kept on drinking. Kept to the safety of the known.

*

The pistons were being pushed at and the treading went perfectly. I felt it where I was supposed to feel it. The sweat was running in phases with the meditative pulse of emerging emotions, writhing and tingling, playing games in the pit of my gut.

That was what it had been like. The dull senses. No pure feelings. Chemical. Fabricated.

It hit me like a punch in the solar plexus. Exactly like that. It had been exactly like that!

"Oh, shit!!!"

*

I thought:

"What was the point of this then? Can you find even one sensible reason for this? So life is more fabulous now, is it? What was wrong with what you had?"

I sank the beer, didn't feel the remorse I was disputing with myself about, not feeling anything for real, really - just stating facts.

"How could you end up doing something this stupid?"

Someone approached me, speaking. I spoke back, shrugged, resumed the binging. Not touched, not untouched.

Something about the whole situation was strange, though. But with the air-bag of liquid substance floating in the can in my hand, that deadened bump didn't amount to anything new coming to mind.

*

The night had been filled with toasts and boasts. Juggling and snuggling with the alcohol. Everything the way it used to be.

The laughs that came from the glass. The conversations that came from far off, detached trails of thought. Feelings that weren't feelings but emerged from the head.

The night had been just like they used to be with only the one common denominator, and everything bound to it. Not a single truly felt moment. Alcohol at the centre of being.

I slowed my tempo. The hammering pulse wasn't triggered solely from my exercise.

It wasn't true! A wide smile started to spread from the soles of my feet. It hadn't happened!

*

"Just one more."

The voice was there, the one I had listened to and obeyed for so, so long. I was used to it, the goal was built in, the road paved. I opened another one. Didn't even raise an eyebrow. Another one. This was the one that would keep me straight.

Are you going to start over? To what end? Will you be doing anything truly challenging, truly courageous, anything pure, ever again? Do you even want to? The questions didn't provoke either feelings of expectation or wonder. The only presence was the monotonous, worn-down, same-same rut. Not safe, not unsafe.

Just sitting there.

But something was askew with this picture. I was in the old territory, without questioning shit. Nothing strange about that then. But I didn't feel real.

Something began picking at me. Something about not really being there. Not really being present.

*

Dawn had broken. Home alone. The morning cup of coffee or two later got me on my bike. To the gym. All in a state of dulled emotion. Too tired to reflect. Not really there.

Yeah, yeah. Get your ass moving, shift into gear. Tread and push, tread and pull, the cross-trainer and I, in a motion of ever-turning circles.

The dream resurfaced. Had had them before. Using dreams. But something was off with this one. The twirl inside increased to a tornado. The dullness dispersed and suddenly I saw it. The thing that had bugged me all night, all the time up to now actually. I saw the emotions.

The emotions that had been there in all those other dreams of using again. The dreams stuffed with feelings of regret and yearning, blended with thoughts bloated with mourning. Saddened while asking the big why, even as I dreamt. "Why was I back in this rut?"

The dreams in which the feelings of regret and remorse, anguish and sorrow were felt. And, upon waking, the unbelievable bursts of relief, of absolute deliverance when I realised that it had been just that, only a dream.

The liberation, the joy!

This dream and morning had been different. Everything had been deadened. As closed off from my spirit as I had been in those days. Always the same, only eroding really. The way I had lived for too many years.

That emotional detachment which I had sought out. That which cuts the edges of all normalcy, empathy. Fabricating delusions of peaks and depths. Not only deafening the insecurity toward that unknown sphere of being in coalition with others which I had feared, but affecting everything true. It had deadened me mercilessly.

What had haunted me this night had been the terrible sense of loss, the absence of the fire of the loving spirit that had become such a significant part of living. Ever since my first day sober. The fuel for true courage that sustained me at being a being in the raw state of existence. The part I had suffocated for all those years.

The power of these swelling emotions gave in when I was suddenly in the eye of the tornado. I could see that I hadn't only been shut off from the unmanageable. The drug had taken it all. Taken the edge of the pulse in me.

The edge of the tingle. The edge of aspiration. The edge of challenge. The edge of healthy fear. The edge of joy and sorrow. The edge of life.

The tears fell when I came to seeing the worst – it had taken the edge of love.

That morning, my subconscious had awoken me in pure terror at this shut-down state. A terror that now slowly, but surely, emerged. My heart had hammered from the sheer, overpowering fear that this hadn't been a dream. I had double and triple-checked myself in my sleep. Sensing that something was terribly wrong. Scared to death that I had actually done this. Relapsed into that blunt existence, and slowly, slowly, in that dreaming phase, the terror had pushed itself up through the dream. Up, up, up, nearing the surface. Finally waking me. Thankfully, thankfully waking me!

*

Just have another sip.

Some people live sober and others, like you, just don't.

One more strengthening swallow. Just one more. That's right!

But something is wrong. Really wrong.

*

In the middle of a motion, I stopped. The smile emerged from the core of my being.

Nothing is written in stone. Not anymore.

I *do* dare to do something different. Something new and fresh with my life.

Thanks to others' outstanding courage, I know that I can do it too.

I tread on. Daring to live. Creating something new under the skies. This had been missing from my dream of patchwork recollections. The whole night had been in search of the wonder of all things new I have in my life today.

*

"A world at your feet", the glitter on the water seemed to say. The silvery surface of the depths in constant movement. Twinkling with all that is new and for ever in transition.

"Keep remembering, then you will always desire to do something new.

Dare to live! Dare to belong!

Dare to aspire to be that which you admire! Belong to the world with a present eye.

Pray for courage and you will always ride the ever new wave on the crest of existence!"

Afterword

One of the many things Emma the Multifaceted One has spoken to me of is that when I lose an eyelash, I ought to wish for something. This happens now and again and even though I am not an overly-superstitious person, I have taken this ritual to heart and, as soon as I discover a little lash on my cheek, I make a wish. From time to time, I try to vary this wish. To sneak in something that is currently on my wanting-to-get-done list.

Especially this urge to wish for something to go my way was clear on three different occasions. The first was when I was going to get my beloved child back home from the family she'd lived in. The second was when I entered into the relationship with my fiancé, and the third time was when I was about to release the Swedish version of "I Only Wanted to Dance", "Jag ville bara dansa".

The gut feeling always made me retract these wishes. I retook them, shoving them back into the lapping waters of the mindful place awash with my desires, and then dutifully reworded the wish before I had even blown away the lash. Saying it as I always end up doing:

"My innermost wish is to be able to have love in my life."

In the most difficult of situations as in the most joyous ones, this is always the spiritual choice that gives the most serenity.

And here I wish to once again remind myself to meditate on love. Asking the question of how boundaries can be loving. Of how to be an asset to my fellow people. Of how to love others as well as myself.

Things have rarely just fallen into my lap and I easily forget all my "revelations" - those delicious trails of thought... Easily spoken and admired, just as easily disputed and forgotten.

If I have learned anything, it is that things only get done if I do them.

Only the things I have done have ever made them real.

I hope I have managed to inspire You, Dear Reader, with -

A desire to realise dreams.

A hope of harvesting from fruitful deeds.

A seeking of courage and discipline to do the loving thing – toward oneself as well as toward the next person.

Finding solutions to what is acceptable for us humans to do toward each other, the animals and the Earth – this is the journey of the true nobility of our world.

Courage and strength are there for all who seek out how to behave lovingly. This is my truth.

Every person makes a difference by making the difference.

With wishes for all the best on Your Journey, Dear Reader!

Thank you for giving me the opportunity to tell my tale.

Yours sincerely,
Lotten Säfström!

There is Strength in Asking for Help

There is help to be found.

For the addict as well as for other people who are harmfully affected by addiction.

There is love, courage and strength in asking for help and advice.

The organisations dealing with these issues are many and can be found all over the world.

Addiction is something that takes no heed of factors such as gender, faith, a persons' role in society or their financial stature.

Unfortunately, substance abuse is a worldwide affliction.

Contact a healthcare centre for more information.

You can always be anonymous when asking. If you live in a small town, there is always the possibility to call another town.

Maybe you can ask someone you trust to look for the answers you seek.

One powerful tool is to search the internet for people or organisations to contact.

When you embark on the quest for finding a solution, you will have taken the first step toward doing something.

However small a step it might seem to you, in reality it is a huge hurdle to overcome -

actually it is a giant leap as you are boosting your willingness to work toward change.

This is true whether you are an addict, a co-dependent or are victimized in any way by this gruesome disorder - and also if you are a professional care-giver.

Remember that taking action towards finding a successful path to recovery is a journey you embark upon out of great love for yourself and those around you.

You are also welcome to send an e-mail with questions and reflections to our Publishing Company.

We will try our best to be of assistance.

Together we are strong!

info@saltodevita.com